Summer's Best

In the Kitchen with Bob

Summer's

Best

Bob Bowersox

Food photographs by Mark Thomas Studio

QVC PUBLISHING, INC.

QVC Publishing, Inc.
Jill Cohen, Vice President and Publisher
Ellen Bruzelius, General Manager
Karen Murgolo, Director of Acquisitions and Rights
Cassandra Reynolds, Publishing Assistant

Produced in association with Patrick Filley Associates, Inc.
Design by Joel Avirom and Jason Snyder
Photography by Mark Thomas Studio
Prop styling by Nancy Micklin
Food Styling by Ann Disrude
Text contributions by Dan Macey

Q Publishing and colophon are trademarks of QVC Publishing, Inc.

Published by QVC Publishing, Inc., 50 Main Street, Mt. Kisco, New York 10549

Manufactured in Hong Kong

ISBN: 1-928998-05-4

First Edition

10 9 8 7 6 5 4 3 2 1

Contents

Introduction

There's just something about summertime, isn't there? Something magical about that period from late May to early September. That time of no school and endless days; baseball, swimming pools and fresh-mown grass; picnics, barbecues and ice cream sundaes covered in chocolate; lazy mornings, afternoons and evenings, when you feel completely justified in not moving a muscle; the buzz of cicadas and the chirp of tree frogs.

Boy, do I love summer! I barely remember growing up in any other season. My childhood was cast in the summer, growing up in Colorado. I remember being six or seven years old, bursting out of the front door at dawn with my sister Maggie, running in the wheat fields 'til noon, then coming back and eating fresh-baked bread probably made with wheat from the very fields we ran through. I learned to cook on a campfire Dad built me in the backyard, burning my first burger as I prepared for my initiation into the Boy Scouts. I experienced Silver Queen corn for the first time during the summer of my tenth birthday, probably one of the greatest gifts my Mom ever gave me.

That's what I remember about summer more than anything else—the food. Anything you want is available in the summer, probably waiting for you on a roadside stand not ten minutes drive from where you're sitting. That Silver Queen, calling your name, begging you to slather it with butter. Broccoli and beans, peaches and apples, watermelon and cantaloupe—at the peak of their freshness and flavor—you can just smell them! Fresh-caught shrimp, clams, tuna and sword-fish from the sea; thick, juicy steaks, plump chicken breasts and pork chops from the land. That's what summer's bounty is to me: great memories and great foods at your fingertips.

So when I thought about putting together a book that took all this seasonal wonder into account, I had to go no further than my own memories for inspiration. Each memory suggested specific recipes and I've collected the best of them here for you.

Like the recipes in Starters—these recall the early summer picnics that Dad would take us on. Being in Colorado, we'd head for the hills with a basket packed with surprises. Dad wouldn't stop at the foothills, though—he'd go all the way to the top of Pike's Peak, above the tree line where the heat of summer gives way to a chill in the air and a whistle in the wind. It was cold enough that you had to keep your hands in your pockets, but Dad made it worth pulling them out to eat. We'd gather around a picnic table and he'd break out the first course—dips that had a little heat to them, like the Horseradish Tomato Dip or the Roasted Garlic and Herb Dip, included here. Mom and Dad taught us to love a good dip, but it had to have a depth of flavor that no jarred or bottled dip could ever achieve.

In my own family, my wife Toni and I are addicted to chilled soups. We fell in love with them on our honeymoon on St. John's in the Caribbean (which took place at the end of a perfect summer, I might add). Incredibly refreshing concoctions like Chilled Zucchini Soup or Watermelon Gazpacho—each a tantalizing first course or a light entrée on their own.

And who doesn't remember family and friends invited over for a late Saturday afternoon barbecue? It was an almost weekly event for us, right on through my teen years. My cousin Ken and my dad would man the grill, with Mom and Aunt Jeanne mixing up marvelous drinks for us all. For your grill, I offer some modern updates on the creations that my family's grill masters would serve up: recipes like Grilled Butterflied Lamb with Mint-Honey Glaze, Chicken with Lime and Tomato Relish, Cajun Burgers with Potatoes and Arugula, Steak and Vegetable Kebabs with Kansas City-Style BBQ Sauce, or Grilled Lemon-Thyme Veal Chops. As for the drinks, try a Watermelon-Ginger Lemonade, a Berry Mint Breeze, or one of my favorites, a Half-and-Half— half lemonade, half ice tea—it'll cool you off instantly.

As for seafood, that will forever be tied to memories of Avalon, New Jersey. Every summer, from the time I was 14 until I was out of college, we would go to a little house at 20th and Avalon Avenue, one block off the beach. Here is where I learned to enjoy clams and oysters, where I came to understand and embrace my mom's total love of shrimp and lobster. We used to prowl the seafood hideaways of the Jersey shore and "borrowed" as many recipe ideas as we paid for. Terrific dishes like Skillet-Grilled Lobster and Corn, Swordfish with Tomato and Olive Confetti, Scallops with Pesto and Salsa, and Shrimp with Green Beans, Tomatoes and Feta Cheese are all included here.

And there were always those great side dishes brought to the gathering by an aunt or a friend. I love Matchstick Zucchini and Summer Squash and Onion Sauté. If you're in the mood for a light salad on a hot evening, look no further than the Grilled Summer Vegetable Salad (spectacular!), the Minted Orzo Salad, or one of my newest favorites, Tabbouleh. It's been said that a great summer meal is defined by its side dishes and its salads...you can't miss with any of those that I've included in *Summer's Best*.

And then there was Lynthwaite's. Owned by an old farmer, Lynthwaite's was a classic ice cream stand out on Route 202, north of Wilmington, Delaware. Mr. Lynthwaite ran it until his death in the late 1960s, and it is sorely missed to this day. He would make his ice cream fresh every day from the milk his few remaining cows would provide. And nearly every night during my last three summers at home before college, our family would drive to Old Man Lynthwaite's and have dessert. For me, summer desserts have forever been defined by the clean, fresh taste of his ice cream, so when I went looking for desserts to include in this book, that memory was the guiding light.

Fresh Mint Chocolate Chip Ice Cream (in honor of Mr. Lynthwaite), Grilled Georgia Peaches à la Mode and the Fourth of July Ice Cream Cake are just some of the cool refreshments included here. And if ice cream isn't what you had in mind, try the Lemon Mousse, the Fresh Berry Shortcake, Strawberry-Rhubarb Pie or Summer Berry Pudding. All have one thing in common— all are fresh, all are refreshing and all are as easy to make as driving out to Old Man Lynthwaite's.

And I guess that's as good a word to describe summer for me as any other—easy. Summer's the season when things should be simple, and the pleasures within easy reach. I hope that the good food included in *Summer's Best,* and the memories it creates, will be that for you—simple and easy. Enjoy!

7

STARTERS

Cherry Tomatoes Stuffed with
Asparagus and Ricotta

Steamed Vegetables with
Spicy Peanut Noodles

Squash Blossom Beignets

Watermelon Gazpacho

Melon and Arugula Salad

Chilled Zucchini Soup

Summer Crudités

Tomato Basil Soup with Lemongrass

Black Bean and Roasted
Yellow Pepper Dip

Minted Cucumber Soup

Tomato Horseradish Dip

Frozen Strawberry Sipper

Roasted Garlic Herb Dip

Berry Mint Breeze

Caponata

Half-and-Half

Green Goddess Dip

Watermelon-Ginger Lemonade

Corn and Cheese Chilies Rellenos

Cherry Tomatoes Stuffed with Asparagus and Ricotta

MAKES 36

BRING THESE TO YOUR NEXT POTLUCK DINNER and watch them disappear almost before you put them down. If you don't have a pastry bag, just use a plastic storage bag and snip off the corner for an easy, no-mess way of filling the tomato cups.

- 1 cup asparagus tips
- 2 tablespoons extra-virgin olive oil
- 36 cherry tomatoes
- 1 garlic clove, minced
- 3 cups ricotta cheese
- 1 cup grated Parmesan cheese
- 1/3 cup chopped fresh basil
- 1/2 teaspoon salt

Bring a small pot of water to a boil. Add the asparagus tips and blanch for 3 minutes. Drain and shock under cold water. Pat dry with paper towels, place in a small bowl and toss with the olive oil.

Using a serrated knife, cut off the bottom 1/8 of each tomato. Scoop out the insides with the small end of a melon scoop. Turn upside down onto paper towels to drain.

Place the garlic, ricotta, Parmesan and basil in the bowl of a food processor. Run the motor until the mixture is smooth.

Turn each tomato upright and sprinkle with the salt. Fill a pastry bag fitted with a plain tube with the ricotta mixture and pipe into the tomato cups. Stuff 2 to 3 asparagus spears into each filled cup.

Squash Blossom Beignets

SERVES 4

CHÈVRE IS THE FRENCH WORD FOR GOAT CHEESE, which is available in most grocery stores packaged in small "logs." You'll probably find it in the store's specialty cheese section. Squash blossoms are available nearly all summer at your local farmer's market or through mail-order catalogues.

1	egg
1	cup cold water
1	cup flour
¼	teaspoon salt
2	garlic cloves, minced
½	onion, diced
2	tablespoons olive oil
¼	cup diced reconstituted sun-dried tomatoes
1	tablespoon chopped fresh sage
16	ounces chèvre
12	squash blossoms, stems removed
	Corn oil
1	cup flour

In a small bowl, beat together the egg and cold water. Gradually add the flour and salt. Set aside for 1 hour.

In a medium-size skillet over low heat, sauté the garlic and onion in the olive oil until soft and translucent, about 5 minutes. Add the sun-dried tomatoes and cook for another 3 minutes. Remove to a medium-size bowl.

Add the sage and chèvre to the sun-dried tomato mixture. Using a rubber spatula, fold until the mixture is well blended. Scrape into a pastry bag fitted with a plain, ½-inch tip. Fill the blossoms with the chèvre mixture and pinch the ends to close.

Bring 3 inches of corn oil to 350°F in a heavy skillet over medium heat. Put the flour in a shallow bowl, next to the egg batter. Give the batter a few stirs if it has separated. Roll each blossom in the flour, dip in the batter and fry, a few at a time, in the oil for 3 to 5 minutes. Turn to brown evenly, then remove with a slotted spoon and drain on paper towels.

Serve with slices of toasted French bread.

Melon and Arugula Salad

SERVES 6

WHAT A GREAT WAY TO BRING HOME A LITTLE bit of the Mediterranean sun! The combination of savory prosciutto—an Italian cured ham—and sweet cantaloupe is a classic Italian first course. When ordering the prosciutto at the deli counter, go for the authentic imported variety, which tends to be leaner and more flavorful than domestic types.

10	cups arugula, rinsed, stems discarded
6	ounces thinly sliced prosciutto
2	tablespoons pine nuts
1	tablespoon red wine vinegar
1	tablespoon balsamic vinegar
1	shallot, minced
1	teaspoon Dijon-style mustard
½	teaspoon salt
½	teaspoon freshly ground pepper
3	tablespoons extra-virgin olive oil
3	tablespoons walnut oil
1½	ounces Parmesan cheese
½	ripe cantaloupe, cut into 1-inch pieces

Wrap the rinsed arugula in paper towels and refrigerate until just before serving.

Place the prosciutto slices on top of each other. Slice in half lengthwise. Cut across into thin strips.

Over medium heat in a small sauté pan, toast the pine nuts until they just begin to brown. Remove immediately from the pan and set aside.

In a small bowl, combine the vinegars, shallot, mustard, salt and pepper. Using a wire whisk, slowly add the oils to form an emulsion.

Place the arugula in a large bowl and toss with ¾ of the vinaigrette. Toss the prosciutto with the remaining vinaigrette. Divide the arugula onto 6 plates, top with equal amounts of the prosciutto. Using a peeler, shave the Parmesan over each salad. Arrange the cantaloupe on top of the arugula.

Sprinkle with the pine nuts.

Summer Crudités

SERVES 6 TO 8

I JUST CAN'T MAKE IT HOME from a stop at a roadside farmstand without sampling the fresh summertime vegetables before they even hit the kitchen counter. Use the dips on pages 15 through 19 to accompany your pick of summer's bounty. Select an assortment of vegetables from the ingredient list, adjusting the quantities to the size and appetite of your group.

½ pound snap beans (green, yellow waxed or purple)

1 baby bok choy (white stems only)

12 baby carrots

½ cucumber

12 thin asparagus

½ large head broccoli

1 head endive

1 fennel bulb

1 small bunch grapes (Concord, Thompson seedless red or green)

2 large bell peppers (green, yellow, orange or red)

12 snow peas or sugar snap

3 to 6 radishes (globe, icicle or rose flesh)

12 baby summer squash or zucchinis

12 green onions

12 cherry tomatoes

2 to 4 cups assorted greens

Wash all the vegetables. Trim the ends of the beans. Twist off the green tops of the carrots and peel lightly. Peel and cut the cucumber into strips or cut into 2-inch sections and hollow out to form cups.

Trim off any tough ends from the asparagus. Trim the broccoli into long florets. Blanch the asparagus and broccoli separately for 2 minutes in boiling water. Drain and immediately rinse under cold running water to cool.

Trim the ends of the endive and separate into leaves. Remove the outer layer of the fennel and cut the bulb crosswise to create curved slices.

Remove the seeds and stems from the bell peppers and cut into thin strips. Break off the stems and remove the strings from the peas. Remove the leaves from the radishes and cut into thin slices. For baby squash trim the stem ends and cut in half on the diagonal. Trim the ends and tops of the green onions.

Create a unique presentation by lining a platter or tray with an assortment of greens, then simply filling different-sized clear glasses with your choice of vegetables, reserving one or more for the dip, and place on the platter.

Black Bean and Roasted Yellow Pepper Dip

MAKES 2 CUPS

I LIKE TO MAXIMIZE THE FLAVORS OF the broiled peppers by covering them for about 10 minutes with aluminum foil once they come out of the oven. This allows the moisture to seep between the pepper and the skin. The blackened skin can then easily be removed.

1 yellow bell pepper, halved, seeded

½ medium onion

1 tablespoon olive oil

1 1-pound can black beans, drained, rinsed

2 garlic cloves, minced

1 teaspoon ground cumin

1 tablespoon finely chopped fresh cilantro

1 tablespoon fresh lemon juice

½ teaspoon salt

½ teaspoon freshly ground pepper

Preheat the broiler. Place the pepper and onion, cut side face down, in a small roasting pan. Drizzle with the olive oil. Place 4 inches below the broiler and cook for 3 to 5 minutes, until the skins begin to blacken. Turn the pepper and onion over and broil for another 2 to 3 minutes. Remove from the oven. When cool enough to handle, cut them into ¼-inch dice and set aside.

Place ⅔ of the black beans in the bowl of a food processor along with the garlic, cumin, cilantro, lemon juice, salt and pepper. Process until very smooth. Scrape into a medium-size mixing bowl and fold in the peppers, onions and remaining black beans. Cover and refrigerate for 2 hours to allow the flavors to meld.

Tomato Horseradish Dip

MAKES 2 CUPS

THEY MAKE HORSERADISH SAUCE NEAR ME in Bucks County, Pennsylvania. The pungent flavors permeate the air outside of the factory and make me crave a taste of this dip. But don't worry about the heat, the yogurt provides a cool sensation while the tomato paste and freshly diced tomato give it a wonderful rosy color.

1   cup plain yogurt

¼   cup mayonnaise

1   tablespoon extra-virgin olive oil

1   teaspoon salt

½   teaspoon freshly ground pepper

1   tablespoon sun-dried tomato paste

1   tablespoon horseradish sauce

2   tablespoons minced green onions

⅓   cup finely diced ripe tomato

In a medium-size bowl, using a wire whisk, combine the yogurt, mayonnaise and olive oil. Add the salt, pepper, sun-dried tomato paste and horseradish sauce. Mix well. Fold in the green onions and tomato, cover and chill until serving.

Roasted Garlic Herb Dip

THIS IS ONE OF MY FAVORITE DIPS BECAUSE when garlic is roasted it takes on a wonderful sweetness that tastes more like caramelized onions than garlic. To make the preparation go even faster, simply cut off the top of a whole head of garlic and roast the entire head. Then squeeze the whole head from the bottom to quickly remove the paste.

1 head garlic, separated into cloves

½ cup sour cream

⅓ cup plain yogurt

2 tablespoons extra-virgin olive oil

1 teaspoon salt

1 teaspoon freshly ground pepper

1 tablespoon finely chopped fresh cilantro

1 tablespoon finely chopped fresh mint

1 tablespoon finely chopped fresh chervil

Preheat the oven to 350°F. Scatter the garlic cloves in a small baking pan. Roast in the oven for 45 minutes. Remove from the oven and when they are cool enough to handle, squeeze the garlic out of the peel and into a medium-size mixing bowl. Using a wire whisk, blend in the remaining ingredients. Cover and chill for at least an hour to let the flavors blend.

Caponata

MAKES 3 TO 4 CUPS

WE HAVE THE ITALIAN REGION OF SICILY TO THANK for originating this terrific recipe. It turns somewhat bland eggplant into a tasty dip or spread that is perfect for toasted, crusty bread. What's really great about this recipe is that it can be made ahead and kept in the refrigerator for weeks.

- 2 cups peeled 1-inch-cubed eggplant
- ¼ cup olive oil
- 1 medium onion, chopped
- ¼ cup chopped celery
- ½ cup chopped green bell pepper
- ½ cup chopped red bell pepper
- 3 garlic cloves, minced
- ½ teaspoon freshly ground pepper
- ½ teaspoon oregano
- 2 medium tomatoes, peeled, chopped with juices
- ½ teaspoon salt
- 2 tablespoons chopped fresh basil
- 2 tablespoons chopped fresh Italian parsley
- ½ cup chopped pitted Kalamata olives
- 2 tablespoons capers, drained

Sauté the eggplant with the olive oil in a large, wide skillet over medium heat for 10 minutes. Stir often to brown on all sides. Add the onion, celery, bell peppers, garlic, pepper and oregano. Sauté for 12 to 15 minutes, until all the vegetables are soft. Add the remaining ingredients, turn the heat to low and simmer gently for 20 minutes.

Serve warm or at room temperature.

Green Goddess Dip

MAKES 1 ½ CUPS

I USED TO ORDER THIS DRESSING WHENEVER I saw it on a restaurant menu but didn't know much about it. After a little research, I found out that this was first served in San Francisco in the 1920s and named in honor of an actor appearing in a play called "The Green Goddess." Now you can make it a star on your table.

1	garlic clove, minced
2	tablespoons finely chopped fresh parsley
2	tablespoons finely chopped fresh chives
2	tablespoons finely chopped fresh tarragon
1	tablespoon finely chopped green onion
2	tablespoons anchovy paste
½	cup mayonnaise
½	cup plain yogurt

Place all of the ingredients in a food processor or blender. Process until smooth and bright green. Place in a small bowl, cover and chill for 1 to 2 hours to allow the flavors to blend.

Corn and Cheese Chilies Rellenos

SERVES 4

ANYONE WHO KNOWS ME KNOWS THAT I love Mexican food. This dish is reminiscent of those jalapeño poppers that you can order in many restaurants, but even better. It's important to remember that the darker the poblano chili, the hotter the pepper. This recipe works best with chilies that are three inches or longer.

8 large fresh poblano chilies

2 cups bottled Mexican-style chili sauce

1 cup chicken broth

Corn oil

⅓ cup flour

3 cups grated mild Cheddar cheese

1 cup fresh corn kernels

4 large eggs

½ teaspoon salt

¼ cup chopped fresh cilantro

Remove the stem of each chili and make a lengthwise slit along the side. Using a spoon, scrape out the seeds and white veins. Place in a roasting pan directly under the broiler. Watch carefully and turn as the skin blisters. Remove from the broiler. When cool enough to handle, using a small, sharp knife, peel off the skin.

Heat the chili sauce and chicken broth in a medium-size saucepot over medium heat. When it simmers, lower the heat and keep it warm.

Bring the corn oil to 375°F in a heavy skillet. Spread the flour onto a plate. In a medium-size bowl, mix the cheese and corn together. Using your hands, form 8 ovals and slip into the chilies. Press the chilies closed, and secure with a toothpick if necessary.

Separate the eggs. Using an electric mixer, beat the whites until they form soft peaks. Gradually add the egg yolks, salt and a tablespoon of the flour from the plate. Roll each stuffed chili in the flour. Shake off the excess and dip into the egg batter. Place in the hot oil and cook 2 or 3 at a time. Turn as the bottom browns, about 3 to 4 minutes. Remove and drain on paper towels and keep warm until all the chilies are fried.

Swirl 2 tablespoons of the chili sauce onto each plate, top with 2 chilies and spoon on the remaining sauce. Sprinkle with the cilantro.

Steamed Vegetables with Spicy Peanut Noodles

SERVES 8 TO 10

MY WIFE TONI LIKES TO MAKE this dish ahead of time for an afternoon backyard barbecue. Once she puts it all together, she pops it in the refrigerator, then about a half hour before serving, she lets it sit out on the kitchen counter to reach room temperature. It's great for picnics, too.

- 1 cup broccoli florets
- 1 red bell pepper, seeded, diced
- ½ pound snow peas, trimmed, cut into 1-inch pieces
- ½ cup fresh or frozen peas
- ⅔ cup smooth or chunky peanut butter
- 4 green onions (white and green parts), chopped
- ⅓ cup chopped fresh cilantro
- 1 tablespoon soy sauce
- 2 to 3 drops Chinese hot pepper sauce
- Juice of 1 lime
- 1 tablespoon salt
- 1 pound spaghetti

Place the broccoli florets in a steamer basket over simmering water and cover. After 10 minutes, add the red pepper, snow peas and peas. Steam for another 5 minutes, then remove from the heat and keep warm.

Place the peanut butter, green onions and cilantro in the bowl of a food processor. Blend well. With the motor running, add the soy sauce, hot pepper sauce and lime juice. If the sauce is too pasty, add a little hot water.

Bring a large pot of water to a boil. Add the salt and the spaghetti. Stir several times while cooking and drain when the pasta is tender, about 10 to 12 minutes.

Place the spaghetti in a wide, shallow bowl and toss with the peanut sauce until the pasta is entirely coated. Add the steamed vegetables and toss again gently.

Watermelon Gazpacho

SERVES 8 TO 10

I LIKE TO CALL THIS "REFRESHMENT IN A BOWL." There is nothing more soothing than cold soup on a hot summer's day. To make this one even more special, try serving the soup in hollowed out cantaloupe halves. Slice off a small piece of the bottom to make sure your cantaloupe bowls don't tip over.

1 small seedless watermelon

1 small yellow-fleshed watermelon or cantaloupe

⅓ cup cider vinegar

3 tablespoons chopped fresh mint

1 cup sliced celery

1 small red onion, diced

1 cucumber, peeled, seeded, diced

1 cup plain yogurt

2 slices white bread, crusts removed, cut into quarters

Mint sprigs for garnish

Cut each melon in half. Remove any seeds. Remove the flesh from half of each melon and cut enough into 1-inch chunks to fill 4 cups. Set aside. Using a melon scoop, form balls of the remaining melon. Cover in a medium bowl and refrigerate until just before serving.

Working in batches, puree the cut-up melon with the remaining ingredients in a blender or food processor until smooth. Place in a sealed container and refrigerate overnight.

To serve, ladle the chilled soup into wide, shallow bowls. Garnish with the melon balls and a sprig of mint.

Chilled Zucchini Soup

SERVES 6

THEY SAY THAT YOU SHOULD EAT WITH your eyes first. Well, this soup, with its swirl of brilliant red pepper in a sea of green, will have your guests wondering whether you are an artist or a cook—and one taste will confirm that you're both!

⅓ cup chopped onion

1 tablespoon olive oil

1 tablespoon ground cumin

2 pounds zucchini, trimmed, thinly sliced

3 cups chicken broth

½ cup heavy cream

1 teaspoon salt

1 6-ounce jar roasted red peppers

8 ounces sour cream

1 tablespoon milk

¼ cup minced fresh cilantro

In a large, heavy skillet over medium heat, sauté the onion in the olive oil for 5 minutes. Add the cumin and cook for another 2 minutes. Stir in the zucchini and broth, cover, lower the heat and cook for 20 minutes. Remove from the heat and allow to cool. Add the cream and puree in batches in a blender. Pour through a strainer, season with the salt, cover and refrigerate for at least 3 hours.

Drain the roasted red peppers and place in a food processor fitted with a steel blade. Puree until smooth. With the motor running, add 2 tablespoons of the sour cream and the milk. Scrape into a small pitcher.

In a small bowl, whisk together the remaining sour cream and the cilantro.

Pour the soup into wide, shallow soup bowls. Pour the red pepper mixture in a zigzag or swirling pattern on the soup. Place a dollop of the cilantro sour cream in the center and serve.

Tomato Basil Soup
with Lemongrass

SERVES 4 TO 6

LEMONGRASS, A POPULAR ASIAN INGREDIENT, IS NOW *appearing on produce shelves in grocery stores all over the country. When using lemongrass, remove and discard the outer stalk and then smash with the back of a chef's knife to release all the flavorful oils. Use the juice of half a lemon if you can't find lemongrass.*

¼ pound loaf Italian bread, thickly sliced

4 cups chicken broth

2 stalks lemongrass, chopped

¼ cup olive oil

2 garlic cloves, minced

2½ pounds very ripe tomatoes, peeled, seeded, chopped

1 teaspoon salt

½ teaspoon freshly ground pepper

½ cup julienned fresh basil

Toast the bread under a broiler until lightly browned on each side, about 4 to 6 minutes. Remove from the oven and tear into small pieces.

In a medium-size pot over medium heat, bring the chicken broth to a boil. Add the lemongrass and simmer for 10 minutes.

In a large, heavy skillet, warm the oil over low heat. Add the garlic and sauté for 2 to 3 minutes. Raise the heat to medium, add the tomatoes, salt and pepper and bring to a simmer. Strain the chicken broth into the tomatoes, discarding the lemongrass. Add the pieces of bread and stir well. Simmer gently for 20 minutes, stirring to break up the bread.

Remove from the heat and allow to cool. Serve at room temperature or chilled. Ladle the soup into wide bowls and sprinkle with the basil.

Minted Cucumber Soup

I HAVE A NEIGHBOR WITH A GARDEN WHO winds up with a bumper crop of cucumbers nearly every summer. And I can always count on finding a couple of cucumbers mysteriously appearing on my back steps for weeks. Now I have a great recipe for his and your extra crop. This soup is a wonderfully refreshing summer starter.

6 kirby (pickling) cucumbers (if unavailable, 3 garden), peeled, chopped

2 teaspoons salt

2 garlic cloves, minced

3 cups plain yogurt

⅓ cup chopped fresh mint

¼ cup chopped fresh basil

In a blender or food processor, puree the cucumber with the salt and garlic. Add the yogurt and process until smooth. Strain through a fine sieve into a bowl, stir in the fresh herbs, cover and chill for 2 to 3 hours. Serve cold in wide, shallow bowls.

Frozen Strawberry Sipper

NEXT TO BLUEBERRY PANCAKES, THIS IS one of my daughter Taylor's favorite fruit recipes. It has the consistency of a milkshake, includes soda like a float and contains more fruit than a smoothie. It's no wonder both kids and adults make a beeline for the blender when we make these.

½ pint lemon sherbet or sorbet

1 pint strawberries, hulled, halved

1 12-ounce can ginger ale

4 large blemish-free strawberries for garnish

Puree the sherbet in a blender until slightly soft. With the motor running, add the halved strawberries and then the ginger ale. Do not blend too long or the daiquiri will become too runny.

Pour the drink into 4 tall glasses. Cut each strawberry almost in half and place on the rim of each glass.

Berry Mint Breeze

SERVES 4

You'll get many requests for the recipe when you serve this drink made up of two fantastic ingredients—frozen berries and peppermint tea. Feel free to create your own signature breeze using other flavored or herbal teas that may be sitting in your pantry.

½ pint raspberries

½ pint blueberries

½ cup water

½ cup sugar

¼ cup minced fresh mint leaves

2 cups water

2 peppermint tea bags

4 mint sprigs for garnish

Place the berries on a flat surface such as a large plate or a cookie sheet. Be sure they are not touching each other and place in the freezer for 2 hours.

Bring the ½ cup water, sugar and mint leaves to a boil in a small pot. Stir until the sugar is dissolved. Remove from the heat and let steep for 10 minutes.

Bring the remaining water to a boil in a small pot. Add the peppermint tea bags, remove from the heat, cover and steep for 10 minutes. When cooled strain the mint syrup into the tea.

Fill 4 tall glasses with ice and drop in the frozen berries. Pour the tea over the ice and berries, garnish with the sprigs of mint and serve.

Half-and-Half

LEMONADE AND ICE TEA, TWO OF summertime's best thirst quenchers—why not combine them? We did and the results will have you serving this delightful twist on two classic beverages right into fall. Or try serving it warm in the winter months for a soothing alternative to coffee.

6 ounces water

¼ cup sugar

⅓ cup fresh lemon juice

6 ounces water

2 tea bags

4 lemon rounds for garnish

Bring the water, sugar and lemon juice to a boil in a small pot over high heat. Stir and boil until the sugar is dissolved.

Bring the remaining water to a boil in a small pot. Add the tea bags, cover, remove from the heat and allow to steep for 10 minutes.

Remove the tea bags. Add the lemon syrup and stir well. Let sit until room temperature. Fill 4 tall glasses with ice and pour the mixture over the ice. Using a sharp knife, make a small cut into each lemon round and secure on the lip of each glass.

Watermelon-Ginger Lemonade

WHEN I WAS A KID, TRUCKS FULL OF the juiciest watermelons used to dot the roadside. I remember running barefoot—trying to avoid the hot pavement as much as I could – to help my mom pick the perfect watermelon. With this recipe, there is no excuse not to select the biggest one, serving up half in slices and making this delicious drink out of the rest.

¼ cup chopped gingerroot

¼ cup fresh lemon juice

⅓ cup honey

½ cup cold water

3 cups chopped seeded watermelon

2 cups crushed ice

Place the ginger, lemon juice and honey in a small saucepot. Bring to a boil, stir, cover and allow to steep for 10 minutes. Remove the cover, add the cold water and cool.

Place the watermelon and crushed ice in a blender. Process until smooth. Slowly strain the ginger syrup into the blender and mix well. Pour into tall glasses and serve.

MAINS

Cajun Burgers with Potatoes
and Arugula

Grilled Pork Tenderloin and
Peppered Peaches

Grilled Pork Chops with
Apple Chutney

Grilled Butterflied Lamb with
Mint-Honey Glaze

Grilled Lemon-Thyme Veal Chops

Medallions of Beef with
Mixed Pepper Chutney

Grilled London Broil
Steak Salad

Curried Lamb and Squash Kebabs

Steak and Vegetable Kebabs with
Kansas City-Style BBQ Sauce

Cajun Fried Chicken with
Mustard Sauce

Tandoori-Style Chicken and Summer
Vegetable Kebabs

Chicken Nuggets Provençale
and Peppers Julienne

Chicken with Lime and Tomato Relish

Pesto-Stuffed Chicken Thighs

Thai Grilled Chicken Noodle Salad

Chicken with Mango and Asparagus

BBQ Turkey Club Salad

Toni's Turkey-Stuffed Peppers

Swordfish with Tomato and Olive Confetti

Sicilian-Style Grilled Tuna Spaghetti

Poached Salmon and Asparagus
with Black Beans and Corn

Scallops with Pesto and Salsa

Shrimp with Green Beans, Tomatoes
and Feta Cheese

Skillet-Grilled Lobster and Corn

Fettuccine with Tomato-Mint Sauce

Confetti Primavera Pasta Salad

Grilled Pizza Margherita

Penne with Bacon, Tomatoes
and Romano

Zucchini and Tomato Omelet

Grilled Greek Salad

Spicy Vegetable Fritters

Curried Stir-Fry

Cajun Burgers with Potatoes and Arugula

SERVES 4

BURGERS ON A BUN CAN GET pretty boring. Why not try serving burgers over arugula and potatoes? To make your own Cajun mustard, simply add some hot spices or even Chesapeake Bay-type seasoning to Dijon-style mustard.

And while I prefer the purple potatoes for this recipe, those small fingerling or even new potatoes will do just fine, too.

1 pound small purple potatoes, scrubbed, thinly sliced into rounds

1 egg, beaten

1 cup soft breadcrumbs

1 teaspoon Cajun seasoning

1 pound ground beef

1 pound small arugula leaves, stems removed

1 ripe tomato, diced

¼ cup Cajun-style mustard

Spread the potato slices in a steamer basket and place over simmering water. Cover and steam for 10 to 15 minutes, until they are opaque and just fork tender. Remove to a plate, cover with a damp towel and keep warm.

In a medium-size mixing bowl, combine the egg, breadcrumbs and Cajun seasoning. Add the beef and mix well. Shape into 4¾-inch patties. Cover and refrigerate for 15 minutes.

Rinse the arugula and discard any yellowing leaves. Dry well with paper towels and arrange on 4 plates. Arrange the potato slices in a 5-inch circle on the arugula.

Broil or barbeque the burgers, 3 inches from the heat, for 5 minutes on each side. Remove to the bed of arugula and potatoes, and sprinkle with the diced tomato. Serve with a dollop of Cajun-style mustard on the side.

Grilled Pork Tenderloin and Peppered Peaches

SERVES 6

MOST OF YOU HAVE HEARD ME SPEAK of my dad's love of cooking with spirits. He'd add bourbon, wine or flavored liqueurs to any dish, just to see what happened. And most times, he'd have a winner. Simmering peaches in bourbon would have been right up his alley. And don't worry about the alcohol content...most of that burns off when you cook it.

½ cup peach preserves

¼ cup bourbon or peach nectar

3 tablespoons white wine vinegar

½ teaspoon hot pepper sauce (such as Tabasco) or more to taste

Salt and freshly ground pepper to taste

2 tablespoons olive oil (preferably fruity extra-virgin oil)

2 pork tenderloins (1½ to 2 pounds total)

3 ripe but firm peaches, peeled, pitted, halved

Freshly ground pepper

In a small saucepan, combine the preserves, bourbon and vinegar. Simmer over medium-low heat, stirring often, until lightly thickened, 5 to 7 minutes. Stir in the pepper sauce, salt and pepper to taste. *(The sauce can be made 2 weeks ahead and refrigerated. Reheat before using.)*

Prepare a medium-hot charcoal fire or bring the grill to a medium-high heat. Brush the pork with about 1 tablespoon of the oil, then season with the salt and pepper. Grill the pork, turning once or twice, for 10 minutes. Meanwhile, brush the peach halves with the remaining oil and season generously with pepper.

Brush the pork with some of the sauce and grill, turning occasionally, 10 minutes more. Brush the peaches with the sauce and grill, turning the peaches and pork once or twice and brushing with more sauce, until the peaches are softened and tinged with gold and the pork is no longer pink in the center, 2 to 4 minutes.

To serve, slice the pork into ½-inch medallions and arrange around a peach half on each plate.

Grilled Pork Chops with Apple Chutney

SERVES 4

WHEN I WAS A KID, Dad would handle the pork chop duty whenever Mom planned them for dinner. He was Pennsylvania Dutch, and the only way he'd eat them was baked on a bed of sauerkraut. Now, that was fine with me—I loved sauerkraut. But my wife Toni isn't crazy about it. She loves a good chutney though, so I came up with this gourmet, restaurant-type of dish for her. What's interesting about it is the addition of the nutmeg...there's almost an apple pie flavor to the dish that you don't expect. Don't you just love surprises?

- 4 center cut loin pork chops
- 1 teaspoon salt
- ½ teaspoon freshly ground pepper
- 2 to 3 tablespoons olive oil
- 4 tablespoons unsalted butter
- 1 large onion, sliced
- 2 garlic cloves, minced
- 4 to 5 tart apples, peeled, cored, thinly sliced
- 1 teaspoon ground nutmeg or freshly grated
- 3 tablespoons balsamic vinegar

Pat dry the pork chops with paper towels. Sprinkle with the salt and pepper and brush with the 1 tablespoon of olive oil.

Melt the butter in a large, heavy skillet over medium heat. Add the onion and garlic and sauté for 5 minutes. Add the apples and nutmeg and stir well. If the mixture seems too dry, add a tablespoon or 2 of olive oil. Cook slowly for 15 to 20 minutes, until the apples and onion begin to brown.

Bring a grill to a medium-high heat. Place the pork chops on the grill, 4 inches from the heat. Cook for 5 to 7 minutes per side, depending on the thickness of the chops. Remove from the heat and keep warm.

Add the balsamic vinegar to the apple mixture and raise the heat to high. Bring to a boil and cook until the vinegar is reduced by half.

Place the chops on individual plates or a serving platter and top with a heaping spoonful of the apple chutney.

Grilled Butterflied Lamb with Mint-Honey Glaze

SERVES 4 TO 6

WHEN I WAS GROWING UP, Mom would make lamb once a week or so. She'd roast it and serve it with mint jelly. We'd lick the plates clean. Now that I've got my own house, and a wife who likes to experiment in the kitchen, we've taken Mom's traditional dish and spruced it up a bit. Glazes are a terrific way to add flavors without a lot of extra ingredients or work. And the combination of mint and honey is terrific!

If you want, reserve some of the glaze or double the amount to make a dipping sauce for the lamb.

4	pounds leg of lamb, boned, butterflied
1	tablespoon coarse salt
2	teaspoons freshly ground pepper
¼	cup honey
2	tablespoons Dijon-style mustard
1	tablespoon corn oil
2	tablespoons lemon juice
⅓	cup chopped fresh mint

Trim off any excess fat from the lamb. Sprinkle the flesh side with the salt and pepper. In a small mixing bowl, whisk together the honey, mustard, oil, lemon juice and mint. Using a rubber spatula, spread the glaze all over the lamb.

Bring a grill to a medium-high heat or, if using a broiler, preheat to medium-high. Place the lamb, fat side up, on the barbecue, 4 inches away from the heat, and cover. If cooking under a broiler, lay the lamb on a rack placed in a large roasting pan and place 4 inches below the broiler. Cook the lamb for 10 to 12 minutes and turn over. Barbecue, or broil for another 10 to 12 minutes and remove to a carving board. Allow the meat to rest for 10 minutes before cutting.

Grilled Lemon-Thyme Veal Chops

SERVES 4

WHEN VEAL CHOPS WERE SERVED at my house growing up, I knew it was a special occasion— usually presents would be handed out and cake would be served. But with a simple herbed lemon marinade and a quick toss on the grill, veal chops can make any meal a special occasion. And do grill the lemons, they add a unique touch to the presentation.

- 2 lemons
- 2 tablespoons olive oil
- 1 tablespoon chopped fresh thyme or 1 teaspoon dried
- 4 center cut veal loin chops
- Salt and freshly ground pepper to taste
- 4 thyme sprigs for garnish (optional)

Cut 1 of the lemons into 8 crosswise slices. Grate ½ teaspoon of peel from the remaining lemon, then squeeze 1 tablespoon of juice. In a small dish, combine the lemon peel, juice, olive oil and chopped thyme. Season the veal with salt and pepper, then brush with some of the lemon mixture. Let stand for 10 minutes at room temperature or refrigerate for up to 3 hours.

Prepare a hot charcoal fire or bring the grill to a high heat. Grill the chops, turning once or twice and brushing with more of the lemon mixture, until no longer pink, about 15 minutes total.

A few minutes before the veal is done, brush the lemon slices with some of the lemon mixture and grill, turning once, until lightly charred and softened, 1 to 2 minutes.

Serve the veal topped with the grilled lemon slices, and garnished with the thyme sprigs, if desired.

Medallions of Beef with Mixed Pepper Chutney

SERVES 4

WHILE STEAK SAUCES ARE FINE to flavor steak, I like to make my own savory, chunky chutney—a condiment of Indian origin that gives meat a nice kick. I normally like to serve the chutney on the side, which allows guests to decide just how much heat they want to add to their filet.

⅔ cup water

¼ cup sugar

2 tablespoons cider vinegar

12 large jalapeño peppers, seeded, thinly sliced

½ cup thinly sliced onion

2 teaspoons mustard seeds

½ cup matchstick-size red bell pepper

½ cup thinly sliced carrots

2 tablespoons chopped fresh cilantro

8 ½-inch-thick slices beef tenderloin

½ teaspoon salt

½ teaspoon freshly ground pepper

2 teaspoons vegetable oil

Cilantro sprigs for garnish

Combine the water, sugar and vinegar in a small saucepot and bring to a boil over high heat. Add the jalapeños, onion, mustard seeds, red pepper, carrots and cilantro and stir for 2 minutes. Keep warm or allow to cool and refrigerate for later use.

Sprinkle the beef slices with the salt and pepper. Lightly brush a large, nonstick skillet with the oil and heat over high heat. Add the beef and sear until brown on both sides, about 2 minutes per side.

Place 2 medallions on each of the plates, top with either warm or chilled chutney and garnish with the cilantro sprigs.

Grilled London Broil Steak Salad

4 SERVINGS

LIKE SO MANY OF YOU, I own one of those indoor grills. I've found mine to be invaluable, both in the summer when the weather prevents outdoor grilling and in the winter when it's too cold to venture outside. London broil is one recipe that works well both inside and out. Tossing it into a salad creates an entire meal in minutes.

½ cup olive oil

3 tablespoons red wine vinegar

1 tablespoon Dijon-style mustard

1 tablespoon chopped fresh thyme or 1 teaspoon dried

1 tablespoon chopped fresh marjoram or 1 teaspoon dried

½ teaspoon freshly ground pepper

2 garlic cloves, chopped

1 pound beef flank steak or top round cut (such as London broil)

6 cups torn romaine lettuce

2 medium tomatoes, cut in wedges

½ cup thin shavings Parmesan or Romano cheese

In a small bowl or glass measuring cup, whisk together the oil, vinegar, mustard, thyme, marjoram, pepper and garlic. Place the meat in a shallow dish just large enough to hold it flat. Pour half of the marinade over the meat, turning to coat the meat on both sides. Cover and refrigerate for at least 6 hours and up to 24 hours, turning occasionally. Reserve the remaining marinade to use as a vinaigrette.

Prepare a hot charcoal fire or bring the grill to a high heat. Remove the meat from the marinade and pat dry on paper towels.

Grill the meat, turning once, to desired degree of doneness, about 12 minutes for rare and about 15 minutes for medium. Let the meat rest for 5 minutes, then slice thinly across the grain.

Toss the lettuce with most of the reserved vinaigrette and divide among 4 plates. Arrange the meat over the lettuce and surround with the tomatoes. Drizzle with the remaining vinaigrette. Sprinkle with the cheese shavings.

Curried Lamb and Squash Kebabs

SERVES 4

To me, lamb always tastes best when it is marinated. I like to use coconut milk, which can either be found in the international section or where drink mixers are stored in your local supermarket. The coconut and curry combine to give the lamb a real tropical punch. Be sure to skewer the zucchini through both sides of the skin to assure it doesn't fall off during grilling.

1 cup canned cream of coconut

3 tablespoons lime juice

2 teaspoons curry powder

1 teaspoon grated lime peel

½ teaspoon salt

¼ teaspoon cayenne pepper

1 pound boneless leg of lamb, cut into 1- to 1½-inch chunks

2 medium-small zucchinis (8 to 10 ounces total), cut into 1- to 1½-inch chunks

4 long or 8 short metal skewers

In a shallow dish just large enough to hold the meat, stir together the cream of coconut, lime juice, curry powder, lime peel, salt and cayenne. Add the meat, stirring to coat completely. Cover and refrigerate for at least 1 hour or up to 6 hours.

Prepare a hot charcoal fire or bring the grill to a high heat. Add the zucchini to the lamb in the marinade, stirring to coat well. Thread the meat and zucchini onto 4 long or 8 short metal skewers, alternating the lamb and vegetables on each skewer.

Grill, turning once or twice until the lamb is browned on the outside but still pink on the inside, and the zucchini is lightly charred and tender, about 5 minutes.

Steak and Vegetable Kebabs with Kansas City-Style BBQ Sauce

SERVES 4

I THINK OF ALL MY VIEWERS AS part of my extended family. So, I'd like to share my formerly secret recipe for barbecue sauce with you. What's really great is how quick it is to make yet how it still retains an intense flavor—like that of other famous Kansas City sauces. It can keep in the refrigerator. It's great for barbecue chicken, too.

- 2 tablespoons vegetable oil
- 1 large onion, finely chopped
- 4 large garlic cloves, minced
- 4 cups ketchup
- ¾ cup cider vinegar
- ¾ cup firmly packed dark brown sugar
- ¼ cup dark molasses
- 2 tablespoons dry mustard
- 1 teaspoon cayenne pepper
- 1 teaspoon white pepper
- 2 teaspoons chili powder
- ¼ cup Worcestershire sauce
- 1½ teaspoons ground cumin
- 8 8-inch wooden skewers
- 2 8-ounce strip steaks, cut into 1-inch cubes
- 1 medium fennel bulb, cut into 2-inch pieces
- 1 pound button mushrooms
- 3 cups cooked white rice

Warm the oil in a heavy, 3-quart saucepot over medium heat. Add the onion and garlic and cook for 7 to 10 minutes, stirring often. Do not allow the onion to brown. Add the next 10 ingredients and stir well. Heat slowly, then simmer for 30 minutes over low heat.

Preheat the broiler, or if barbecuing, bring the grill to a high heat. Assemble the kebabs, alternating the meat with the vegetables. Leave an inch of space on either end of the skewers. Brush with liberal amounts of the sauce, covering all sides of each kebab. Barbecue or broil 3-inches from the heat for 10 minutes. Turn the kebabs several times as each side browns.

Serve on a bed of white rice with extra sauce on the side.

Cajun Fried Chicken with Mustard Sauce

SERVES 4

I OFTEN GET THE QUESTION, "What's a great recipe to make when the grandkids come to visit?" Well, here's one that should make all grandparents' lives a bit easier and the grandchildren even happier. By using chicken tenders, you cut down on cooking time and make bite-size pieces perfect for little fingers to handle.

2 tablespoons salt

2 tablespoons freshly ground pepper

1 tablespoon cayenne pepper

3 pounds chicken tenders

Corn oil for frying

2 cups flour

½ cup coarse mustard

⅔ cup mayonnaise

1 tablespoon hot horseradish sauce

3 to 4 drops hot chili oil

In a small bowl, blend the salt, pepper and cayenne. Pat dry the tenders with paper towels. Coat the chicken with the rub, cover and refrigerate for 2 to 3 hours.

Bring 2 inches of corn oil to 375°F in a deep, heavy skillet. Roll the chicken in the flour and fry a few at a time so as not to crowd the skillet, turning as each side browns, for 5 to 6 minutes. Remove from the oil to drain on paper towels. Keep warm in the oven until they are all fried.

In a small bowl, whisk together the mustard, mayonnaise, horseradish sauce and chili oil.

Serve the chicken on individual plates along with a dollop of the sauce, or on a platter with a dish of sauce in the center.

Tandoori-Style Chicken and Summer Vegetable Kebabs

SERVES 4

A TANDOORI IS A FASCINATING clay oven used in India in which the heat is maintained at about 500°F. Obviously, meat cooks very fast. Duplicating the flavors of an authentic tandoori works best when cooked over very hot coals or a hot grill. The cumin, coriander and turmeric add even more of an Indian flavor.

1½   cups plain yogurt

1   tablespoon lemon juice

1   tablespoon chopped gingerroot

2   garlic cloves, finely chopped

2   teaspoons ground cumin

½   teaspoon ground coriander

½   teaspoon ground turmeric

½   teaspoon salt

¼   teaspoon cayenne pepper

1   pound skinless boneless chicken thighs, cut into 1- to 1½-inch chunks

1   red bell pepper, cut into 1½-inch chunks

8   green onions, trimmed to leave 2 inches of green

1   yellow summer squash, cut into ½-inch rounds

4   long or 8 short metal skewers

In a shallow dish just large enough to hold the chicken, combine the yogurt and lemon juice. Add the ginger, garlic, cumin, coriander, turmeric, salt and cayenne to the yogurt mixture and stir together. Add the chicken, stirring to coat completely. Cover and refrigerate for at least 1 hour or up to 4 hours.

Prepare a medium-hot charcoal fire or bring the grill to a medium-high heat. Remove the chicken from the marinade, then add the bell pepper, green onions and squash to the marinade left in the dish. Stir to coat. Thread the chicken and vegetables onto the metal skewers.

Grill, turning occasionally, until the chicken is cooked through and the vegetables are tender, 6 to 8 minutes.

Chicken Nuggets Provençale and Peppers Julienne

SERVES 4

GROWNUPS LIKE—NO, LOVE—chicken nuggets too. After all, who's the one who really cleans the kids' plates? Dad? Mom? Well, here's a recipe for creating your very own adult chicken nuggets flavored with herbes de Provence. If you don't have any on hand, make your own by combining dried basil, fennel seed, marjoram, rosemary, sage and thyme.

2	pounds skinless boneless chicken breasts, cut into 1-inch pieces
½	cup flour
2	tablespoons herbes de Provence
¼	cup olive oil
½	red bell pepper, julienned
½	green bell pepper, julienned
½	yellow bell pepper, julienned
2	garlic cloves, chopped
2	tablespoons olive oil
1	teaspoon salt

Pat dry the chicken with paper towels. In a wide bowl, mix the flour with the spices. Heat the ¼ cup of oil in a large, heavy skillet over medium-high heat. Dredge the chicken in the flour mixture and when the oil is hot, but not smoking, add the chicken. Work in batches so as not to crowd the pan. Turn as each side browns. Cook until each side is a deep golden and each piece is cooked through, about 5 minutes. Keep warm in the oven.

In another heavy skillet over medium heat, sauté the peppers and garlic in the 2 tablespoons of oil until tender, about 3 to 5 minutes. Sprinkle with the salt and toss well.

Arrange the chicken in the center of a serving platter or on individual plates and surround with the peppers.

Chicken with Lime and Tomato Relish

When tomatoes are in season, I could eat them morning, noon and night. Combining them with limes in a quick relish creates a cool salsa, perfect for anyone who likes fresh flavors but not the usual heat of jalapeños. One quick way to tenderize the chicken is to wrap the breasts in plastic wrap and then pound them with a mallet or rolling pin.

In a large, heavy skillet over medium-high heat, brown the chicken in the olive oil for 3 to 5 minutes on both sides. Add the white wine, cover and simmer for 5 minutes.

In a medium-size, heavy saucepot, combine the remaining ingredients. Bring to a full boil over high heat and stir well.

Place the chicken on a serving platter and cover each breast with a spoonful of the relish.

4   skinless boneless chicken breasts, pounded to ¼-inch thick

2   tablespoons olive oil

1   cup dry white wine

2   limes, thinly sliced, seeded, each slice quartered

4   large ripe tomatoes, cored, chopped

1   large onion, chopped

1   medium green bell pepper, seeded, chopped

1   garlic clove, finely chopped

1½ teaspoons mustard seeds

½   teaspoon celery seeds

¼   teaspoon ground cloves

1   teaspoon salt

2   tablespoons sugar

½   cup white vinegar

Pesto-Stuffed Chicken Thighs

SERVES 4

WHEN EVERYONE ELSE IS REACHING FOR *the white meat, I go for the thighs, which I think contain the most flavor. Apparently I'm not the only one, since boneless thighs can now be found in more supermarkets. While pesto makes a perfect sauce for pasta, it also shines as a stuffing. For you white meat lovers, this recipe works equally well with boneless chicken breasts.*

4 skin-on boneless chicken thighs (about 1 pound)

4 tablespoons prepared basil pesto

1 tablespoon olive oil

Salt and freshly ground pepper to taste

Fresh basil leaves for garnish (optional)

Prepare a medium-hot charcoal fire or bring the grill to a medium-high heat. Use your fingers to loosen the chicken skin, then use your hands to flatten the chicken to an even thickness of about ¾ inch. Smear 1 tablespoon of pesto under the skin of each chicken thigh. Rub the outside of the chicken with the olive oil, then season with the salt and pepper.

Grill the chicken, turning once or twice, until the juices run clear, 12 to 17 minutes. Serve garnished with the basil leaves, if desired.

Thai Grilled Chicken Noodle Salad

SERVES 4

I'VE LEARNED A GREAT TRICK to make meal preparation go faster. Mix up a flavorful concoction that doubles as a marinade and a sauce. That's what I've done here with one of my favorite summertime dishes. I know first hand that this Asian noodle salad is a real crowd pleaser. You only have to watch how fast my brother Paul consumes this dish at picnics!

½ cup chopped green onions

½ cup peanut oil

¼ cup lime juice

¼ cup chopped fresh basil

¼ cup chopped fresh mint

2 tablespoons Thai fish sauce

2 large garlic cloves, chopped

2 teaspoons chopped gingerroot

1 small jalapeño pepper, finely chopped

1 pound skinless boneless chicken breasts

12 ounces Asian noodles or American vermicelli or thin spaghetti

¼ cup sliced radishes

1 cup coarsely chopped yellow bell pepper

In a small bowl, stir together ¼ cup of the green onions, the oil, lime juice, basil, mint, fish sauce, garlic, ginger and jalapeño. Use your hands to flatten the chicken to an even thickness of about ¾ inch. Place the chicken in a shallow dish and pour ⅓ of the marinade over the chicken, reserving the remainder to use as a salad dressing. Turn the chicken to coat with the marinade, then cover and refrigerate for at least 1 hour and up to 6 hours.

Prepare a medium-hot charcoal fire or bring the grill to a medium-high heat. Grill the chicken, turning occasionally, until the juices run clear, 10 to 15 minutes. Thinly slice the chicken across the grain.

Cook the pasta in a large pot of boiling, salted water until tender but still firm to the bite. Drain well. Toss the pasta with the reserved marinade, then add the chicken, radishes, bell pepper and the remaining green onions and toss again. Serve warm or at cool room temperature.

Chicken with Mango and Asparagus

SERVES 4 TO 6

MANGO IS ONE OF THOSE INGREDIENTS that remind me of vacations spent with my wife in the Caribbean. This fruit's flavors are like no other, a little sweet and a little spicy in one ripe package. Serve this chicken dish with some white rice tossed with about a quarter cup of sweetened coconut and you will get a real taste of the islands.

2 pounds skinless boneless chicken breasts, cubed

2 tablespoons dry vermouth

1 large egg white, lightly beaten

1 tablespoon cornstarch

1 teaspoon coarse salt

3 tablespoons corn oil

½ cup finely chopped onion

1 garlic clove, minced

1 cup chicken stock, near boiling

1 tablespoon cornstarch

½ cup dry white wine

2 tablespoons oyster sauce

1 tablespoon soy sauce

2 tablespoons corn oil

1 2-inch piece gingerroot, peeled, thinly sliced

½ red bell pepper, seeded, julienned

10 thin asparagus spears, cut into 1-inch pieces

2 ripe mangos, peeled, cut into chunks

½ cup walnut halves

Place the chicken in a shallow pan and toss with the vermouth. Beat together the egg white, cornstarch and salt, pour over the chicken and mix to coat. Fold in 2 tablespoons of the oil, cover and refrigerate for 30 minutes.

Warm 1 tablespoon of oil in a small saucepot over medium heat. Add the onion and garlic and sauté for 5 minutes. Stir in the hot stock. Combine the cornstarch with the white wine, oyster sauce and soy sauce and gradually whisk into the stock mixture. Bring to a boil and stir frequently for 5 minutes.

In a large, heavy skillet, heat 1 tablespoon of corn oil over medium-high heat. Add the marinated chicken and cook, turning the pieces as they brown, for 10 minutes, until they are nearly cooked through. Remove from the pan and keep warm. Add the remaining 1 tablespoon of corn oil and add the gingerroot. Sauté for 1 minute and then add the red pepper and asparagus. Add the sauce, chicken and mango and bring to a gentle simmer for 3 to 5 minutes. Stir in the walnuts and serve.

BBQ Turkey Club Salad

SERVES 4

DINNER WAS ALWAYS AT 5:30 on the dot when I was growing up. Getting dinner on the table at a consistent time in today's fast-paced world is a bit harder. I've tried to come to your rescue with this recipe. Marinate the turkey or chicken breast in the morning. Then a quick grill and a toss with vegetables at the end of the day allows dinner to be on the table in minutes.

1 cup bottled buttermilk ranch dressing

1 pound skinless boneless turkey or chicken breast cutlets

1 large head leaf lettuce, torn

1 cup cherry tomatoes

1 cucumber, peeled, seeded, sliced

4 slices bacon, cooked, drained, crumbled

Pour ½ cup of the dressing in a shallow dish just large enough to hold the turkey, turning to coat both sides. Cover and refrigerate for at least 30 minutes or up to 2 hours. Reserve the remaining dressing.

Prepare a hot charcoal fire or bring the grill to a high heat. Grill the turkey, turning once or twice, until cooked through, about 5 minutes. Thinly slice the turkey across the grain.

Toss the lettuce with most of the reserved dressing. Divide among individual plates. Arrange the turkey on the lettuce, then garnish with the tomatoes and cucumber. Drizzle with the remaining dressing. Sprinkle with the bacon.

Toni's Turkey-Stuffed Peppers

SERVES 4

I LOVE COMING HOME FROM A LONG day at the studio and being hit with the smells of peppers and tomatoes. I immediately know that we are having my wife's often-sought-after stuffed peppers. Always watchful of my waistline, she cuts the calories by using ground turkey instead of ground beef.

1 onion, chopped

1 garlic clove, minced

2 tablespoons olive oil

1 pound ground turkey

1 cup cooked white rice

¾ cup canned crushed tomatoes

2 teaspoons basil

1 teaspoon oregano

⅔ cup grated mozzarella cheese

4 red, green or yellow bell peppers (or a combination)

In a wide skillet over medium heat, sauté the onion and garlic in the olive oil for 3 to 5 minutes. Crumble the turkey into the pan and cook, stirring often, for 5 to 7 minutes. Add the rice, crushed tomatoes, basil and oregano and mix well. Simmer gently for 3 minutes, stir in ⅓ cup of the cheese and remove from the heat.

Preheat the oven to 350°F. Cut the tops off the peppers. Dice up the tops and add to the turkey mixture. Remove the seeds and white fibers from the insides of the peppers. Fill each pepper with the turkey mixture. Top with the remaining cheese and place them in a baking dish which is small enough so that the peppers fit snugly. Place in the oven and bake for 25 to 30 minutes. Remove from the oven and serve immediately.

Swordfish with Tomato and Olive Confetti

SERVES 4

FRESH SWORDFISH IS AVAILABLE FROM spring to early fall. I've always loved just broiling it with some lemon and salt, but because this fish can complement so many other flavors, there's hardly anything you can't do with it. My wife Toni likes me to grill it for her because it adds a whole new layer of flavors. Simmering it in wine is another terrific way to prepare it, because it produces a flaky and flavor-filled fish. Any way you make it, swordfish is a winner.

- 4 1-inch-thick swordfish steaks
- 2 tablespoons olive oil
- 1 cup dry white wine
- 3 ripe tomatoes, seeded, chopped
- ¾ cup sliced pimento-stuffed green olives
- ¾ cup sliced pitted black olives
- ¼ cup drained capers
- ½ cup sliced green onions (white and green parts)
- ⅓ cup fresh lime juice
- ½ cup olive oil
- 1 teaspoon freshly ground pepper
- 2 bunches watercress sprigs, rinsed, dried
- 4 lime wedges

Rinse the fish, pat dry and brush both sides with the 2 tablespoons olive oil. Place a wide skillet over medium-high heat. When hot, add the fish. When it begins to sizzle, about 2 to 3 minutes, flip it over and add the white wine. When the wine begins to simmer, lower the heat, cover and cook for 5 to 7 minutes, until the fish is firm, but still moist in its thickest point.

In a medium-size bowl, combine the tomatoes, olives, capers, green onions, lime juice, ½ cup olive oil and pepper. Toss well.

Arrange the watercress as a bed on each plate. Just as the fish is finishing cooking, add the tomato and olive mixture to the skillet. Cook for just 1 or 2 minutes to heat through. Remove the fish with a slotted spatula onto the watercress. Drain the confetti from the wine liquid and spoon onto the fish.

Sicilian-Style Grilled Tuna Spaghetti

SERVES 4

FRESH FISH HAS ALWAYS BEEN A big part of my summertime diet. And what better place to find a recipe for seafood than sunny Sicily, located at the tip of Italy, surrounded by the warm Mediterranean Sea. The combination of tuna and pasta goes back hundreds of years in Sicily and the great flavors are a testament to why.

¼ cup red or white wine vinegar

2 garlic cloves, chopped

1 tablespoon chopped fresh oregano plus sprigs for garnish or 1 teaspoon dried

1 tablespoon chopped fresh rosemary plus sprigs for garnish or 1 teaspoon dried

¼ teaspoon crushed hot red pepper

2 anchovy fillets, chopped (optional)

10 tablespoons olive oil

1 pound ¾-inch-thick tuna steaks

1 yellow bell pepper, seeded, thickly sliced

1 sweet onion, cut into 8 wedges

4 long or 8 short metal skewers

1 pound spaghetti, freshly cooked, drained

1 cup coarsely diced fresh plum tomatoes

In a small bowl, whisk together the vinegar, garlic, oregano, rosemary, hot pepper flakes and anchovies (if using). Slowly whisk in the oil to blend well. In a shallow dish just large enough to hold the fish, pour about ⅓ cup of the marinade. Add the fish, turning to coat both sides. Refrigerate for at least 30 minutes or up to 2 hours. Remove the fish from the marinade and add the pepper and onion, stirring to coat with the marinade. Thread the pepper and onion onto metal skewers.

Prepare a medium-hot charcoal fire or bring the grill to a medium-high heat. Grill the fish and skewered vegetables, turning once, until the vegetables are softened and the fish is just cooked through, 6 to 9 minutes. Thinly slice the pepper and onion.

Toss the pasta with the remaining marinade, then toss again with the grilled vegetables and tomatoes. Divide the pasta among 4 individual plates or place on a large platter. Arrange the tuna steaks on top. Garnish with the herb sprigs.

Poached Salmon and Asparagus with Black Beans and Corn

SERVES 4

I HAVE ALWAYS LOVED SALMON. There's something about the texture and taste that's the perfect combination for me. I also like the fact that it cooks quickly. This recipe uses an aromatic broth flavored with fresh herbs as a poaching liquid to cook both the salmon and the asparagus—the end result of which is a perfect melding of flavors.

1 cup white wine

2 cups chicken stock

1 shallot, minced

3 garlic cloves, chopped

2 thyme sprigs

1 whole bay leaf

½ teaspoon freshly ground black pepper

4 5-ounce salmon fillets, skins removed

1 pound asparagus, lower stalks trimmed

¼ cup fresh corn kernels

1 cup canned black beans, drained, rinsed

1 tomato, diced

¼ red onion, minced

2 tablespoons serrano pepper, minced

1 tablespoon chopped fresh cilantro

3 garlic cloves, minced

Juice of 1 lime

2 teaspoons balsamic vinegar

1 teaspoon ground cumin

1½ teaspoons hot pepper sauce (such as Tabasco)

2 cups washed fresh spinach leaves, stemmed

1 tablespoon chopped fresh chives

In a large skillet, bring the wine, stock, shallot, garlic, thyme, bay leaf and black pepper to a boil. Add the salmon and asparagus. When the poaching liquid comes to a simmer, lower the heat so it will not boil. Cook for 5 to 7 minutes, until the salmon is opaque and firm. Remove the fish and asparagus with a slotted spatula and keep warm.

In a medium-size bowl, combine the corn kernels, black beans, tomato, onion, serrano pepper, cilantro, garlic, lime juice, balsamic vinegar, cumin and hot pepper sauce. Mix well.

Arrange the spinach leaves on each plate. Place the salmon and asparagus on top and surround with the bean mixture. Sprinkle with the chopped chives.

Scallops with Pesto and Salsa

SERVES 4

MY DAD WAS A BIG PESTO FAN and my mom just loved seafood. This is a recipe that satisfies both my parents' favorites. Then it goes even further to please yet another family member—my brother Paul who is crazy about salsa. You couldn't find a dish any family friendlier at my house if you tried.

2   tablespoons pine nuts

2   cups fresh basil leaves

2   garlic cloves, chopped

½   teaspoon salt

⅓   cup extra-virgin olive oil

1   cup peeled seeded chopped tomatoes

2   tablespoons sliced green onions (green parts only)

1   tablespoon minced jalapeño pepper

2   tablespoons extra-virgin olive oil

1   tablespoon fresh lime juice

½   teaspoon freshly ground pepper

12   to 16 large sea scallops

Sprinkle salt and freshly ground pepper

¼   cup dry vermouth

In a small, heavy skillet over medium heat, sauté the pine nuts for about 3 minutes, until they begin to brown. Remove immediately and place in a blender or the bowl of a food processor.

Add the basil, garlic and salt. Puree until smooth. Slowly add the ⅓ cup of oil to form a thick sauce. Set aside.

Mix the tomatoes, green onions, jalapeño, 1 tablespoon oil, lime juice and pepper in a small bowl. Toss well, cover and refrigerate.

Place a large, heavy skillet over high heat and coat with the remaining oil. When it is very hot, but not smoking, add the scallops, a few at a time, and cook until browned, about 2 to 4 minutes. Turn over and brown on the other side. Transfer to a warm plate and sprinkle with salt and pepper. Add the vermouth and the juices from the scallop plate to the hot skillet. Boil for about 2 minutes, until it reduces to 2 tablespoons. Stir in the pesto sauce.

To serve, place a circle of the pesto sauce in the center of each plate. Place the scallops on the sauce and top each scallop with a small spoonful of the salsa.

Shrimp with Green Beans, Tomatoes and Feta Cheese

SERVES 4

WE'RE ALL VERY BUSY THESE DAYS, so I like to try to come up with recipes where the entire meal can be made within 15 minutes. Luckily, my daughter Taylor is a HUGE fan of shrimp, and they only take minutes to cook. Then you add in the quick simmer of some green beans and tomatoes, and my favorite, feta cheese, and you get an instant meal that pleases everyone.

2 tablespoons olive oil

1 pound medium-size shrimp, peeled, deveined

3 large garlic cloves, minced

1½ pounds fresh green beans, cut into 1-inch lengths

4 cups peeled chopped tomatoes (including juice)

1 tablespoon chopped fresh sage

2 tablespoons dry white wine

2 tablespoons fresh lemon juice

1 cup feta cheese

Hot cooked white rice

In a large, heavy skillet, heat 1 tablespoon of oil over high heat. Add the shrimp and garlic. Cook, stirring often, until the shrimp are pink, about 2 to 3 minutes. Remove the shrimp to a plate.

Add the remaining tablespoon of oil, green beans, tomatoes, sage and wine to the skillet. Bring to a boil, stir and reduce the heat until it simmers gently. Cover and cook for 8 to 10 minutes, until the beans are crisp-tender.

Return the shrimp to the skillet. Stir in the lemon juice and feta. Cook until heated through and serve over hot cooked white rice.

Skillet-Grilled Lobster and Corn

SERVES 4

WARM AND BREEZY SUMMER evenings are a great time to relax with an intimate dinner at home with friends. What could be more perfect on one of those nights than lobster combined with sweet corn? You will really impress your guests when you ignite the bourbon that flavors the rich lobster meat and create a delicious sauce with fresh herbs.

2 tablespoons unsalted butter

2 tablespoons corn oil

4 lobster tails (about 4 pounds), removed from shells

3 cups fresh corn kernels

½ cup bourbon

½ cup dry white wine

1½ tablespoons chopped fresh tarragon leaves

1½ tablespoons chopped fresh chives

Salt and freshly ground pepper to taste

Melt the butter in the corn oil in a large, heavy skillet over medium-high heat. Add the lobster tails and brown on all sides, about 5 to 7 minutes. Remove the lobster from the pan and set aside. Add the corn to the skillet and sauté for 5 to 7 minutes. Add the bourbon and lobster meat and ignite. Shake the pan until the flames die down and then add the wine. Simmer for 3 to 4 minutes and sprinkle with the herbs. Season with salt and pepper. Place a lobster tail in the center of each plate or serving platter and surround with the corn.

Fettuccine with Tomato-Mint Sauce

SERVES 4

FETTUCCINE IS JUST ABOUT my favorite pasta. This pasta holds sauces well due to the tiny ridges and indentations in each strand. And often, the simpler the sauce, the tastier the dish.

That certainly is so in this recipe, where a mixture of tomatoes and mint creates a very fresh and aromatic flavor.

- 4 slices bacon
- 2 tablespoons unsalted butter
- 3 large tomatoes (including juice), chopped
- ¾ cup chopped fresh mint
- ½ teaspoon salt
- ½ teaspoon freshly ground pepper
- 1 pound fettuccine

Fry the bacon in a large skillet over medium-high heat until crisp, about 5 to 7 minutes. Remove and drain on paper towels. Crumble and set aside.

Melt the butter in the bacon fat over medium heat. Add the tomatoes and simmer for 7 to 10 minutes. Stir in the mint and simmer for 2 to 3 minutes. Season with the salt and pepper.

Cook the fettuccine according to the instructions on the package. Drain and toss with the sauce. Sprinkle with the bacon.

Confetti Primavera Pasta Salad

Serves 4 to 6

Primavera is Italian for "spring style" and has come to refer to the use of fresh vegetables in a dish – especially pasta. I like to call this "garden pasta salad" because it allows you to use just about any fresh-picked summer vegetable from your garden. It works best when all the vegetables are cut to the same size.

1 pound angel hair pasta

2 tablespoons extra-virgin olive oil

1 carrot, cut into small dice

1 cup finely diced fennel (white part only)

1 red bell pepper, seeded, cut into small dice

1 green bell pepper, seeded, cut into small dice

1 yellow bell pepper, seeded, cut into small dice

3 green onions (white and green parts), cut into ½-inch pieces

½ cup fresh peas

2 tablespoons chopped fresh oregano

⅓ cup extra-virgin olive oil

3 garlic cloves, sliced

Freshly grated Parmesan cheese

Cook the pasta according to the directions on the package. Drain and run under cold water to stop the cooking and rinse off the excess starch. Toss in a large bowl with the 2 tablespoons of olive oil. Cover and refrigerate.

Layer the vegetables in the order listed in the basket of a steamer. Place over boiling water, cover and steam for 7 to 10 minutes. Remove to a medium-size bowl and toss with the fresh oregano.

While the vegetables are steaming, warm the ⅓ cup extra-virgin olive oil over medium heat in a small skillet. Add the garlic slices and sauté until they begin to brown, about 4 minutes. Pour immediately into a cup and toss with the vegetables as soon as they are cooked. Cover and refrigerate.

Before serving, toss the pasta and vegetables together. Serve with the Parmesan cheese on the side.

Grilled Pizza Margherita

SERVES 4

BE SURE TO GET THE ENTIRE FAMILY to rally around the grill for this recipe. Everyone can make his or her own personal pizza in only minutes. The kids will especially get a kick out of coming up with their own favorite toppings to turn refrigerated pizza dough into what I'm sure will become a backyard classic.

- 4 tablespoons olive oil
- 3 garlic cloves, chopped
- ¼ teaspoon crushed hot red pepper
- 1 10- to 12-ounce tube or package refrigerated pizza dough
- 2 cups seeded coarsely chopped fresh plum tomatoes
- 2 tablespoons chopped fresh basil plus ¼ cup basil leaves for garnish
- 1 cup (4 ounces) shredded mozzarella or Provolone cheese
- 2 tablespoons grated Parmesan cheese

Prepare a medium-hot charcoal fire or bring the grill to a medium-high heat.

In a small dish, stir together the oil, garlic and red pepper. Roll or pat the pizza dough onto a baking sheet to make a rough 14-inch square. Brush the dough with about 1 tablespoon of the oil mixture. Cut the dough into 4 square pieces of equal size. Turn the dough over and brush the bottom with a total of about 1 tablespoon additional oil mixture. In a small bowl, combine the remaining oil mixture with the tomatoes and chopped basil. In another bowl, toss together the mozzarella and Parmesan cheese.

Use a spatula to slide the pizza squares directly onto the grill. Grill until grill marks appear and the bottom of the dough is pale golden, 2 to 3 minutes. Use the spatula to turn the pizza squares over. Immediately sprinkle the tomato mixture on top and then sprinkle with the cheeses. Cover the grill and cook until the crust is golden with grill marks and the cheese is melted, about 2 minutes. Garnish with basil leaves and serve.

Penne with Bacon, Tomatoes and Romano

SERVES 4 TO 6

EVERYONE KNOWS HOW WELL the flavors of bacon and tomato go together when you bite into a bacon, lettuce and tomato sandwich. Well, combine that with some delicious Italian cheese, a little garlic, the heat of a jalapeño pepper and serve it over pasta, and you have nearly all of my ideal foods combined into one dish.

1 cup chopped bacon

1 large garlic clove, sliced

1 onion, chopped

2 tablespoons extra-virgin olive oil

½ jalapeño pepper, seeded, chopped

3 tomatoes (including juices), chopped

½ teaspoon salt

1 pound penne

¾ cup grated Romano cheese

In a large skillet over medium heat, sauté the bacon, garlic and onion in the olive oil for 5 minutes. Add the jalapeño pepper and tomatoes and stir well. Simmer for 5 minutes. Season with the salt.

Cook the penne as instructed on the package. Drain and toss with the sauce and Romano cheese.

Zucchini and Tomato Omelet

SERVES 4

AT MY HOUSE, OMELETS ARE NOT just for breakfast. We love them for lunch and even dinner. And this is not your ordinary omelet. Here I've layered the herbed eggs and vegetables to enhance the flavors of both. Monterey Jack cheese is added to create what my daughter likes to call an egg lasagna.

2	tablespoons olive oil
½	pound zucchini, diced
¼	cup finely chopped mushrooms
1	cup peeled seeded chopped tomatoes
¼	cup chopped fresh basil
8	eggs
2	tablespoons water
2	tablespoons chopped fresh chives
1	tablespoon chopped fresh parsley
¼	teaspoon salt
½	teaspoon freshly ground pepper
4	tablespoons unsalted butter
1½	cups grated Monterey Jack cheese

Pour the olive oil into a large skillet set over medium heat. Add the zucchini and cook for 3 minutes. Stir in the mushrooms and cook for another 3 minutes. Add the tomatoes and basil. When it begins to simmer, cover and remove from the heat.

In a medium-size bowl, beat the eggs and water. Sprinkle in the chives, parsley, salt and pepper and mix well.

Melt half the butter in a large, heavy skillet over medium-high heat. Move the pan around so that the butter coats the entire bottom of the pan and halfway up its sides. Pour in half the egg mixture and tilt the pan so the eggs spread over the entire bottom of the pan. When the eggs begin to set, gently loosen the edges of the omelet with a spatula. Shake the pan a few times and using fingers, lift the omelet and flip over. Cook for 2 to 3 minutes and then slide onto a large plate. Keep warm in the oven.

Melt the remaining butter in the skillet over medium-high heat. Pour in the other half of the eggs and slowly tilt to evenly cover the bottom of the pan. Sprinkle the cheese over all the eggs and then spoon on the tomato mixture. Immediately slide the first omelet on top of the filled one and press down gently. Slide the entire omelet onto a cutting board and cut into 4 wedges. Lift with a spatula onto each plate and serve with warm English muffins.

Grilled Greek Salad

SERVES 4

SOMETHING HAPPENED TO ME WHEN I turned 40 years old. Before that fateful day, I couldn't stand feta cheese – the idea of it, the smell of it, the taste of it. But after that milestone birthday, I happened to try a bite of a Greek salad, and was suddenly caught by the wonderful overtones that the feta gave it. I've been hooked ever since. Toss it with a little romaine lettuce and grilled veggies, throw in some Kalamata olives, and you have a robust, tangy salad that will become a lunch or dinner favorite.

½ cup olive oil

2 garlic cloves, chopped

1 tablespoon chopped fresh mint plus sprigs for garnish

1 tablespoon chopped fresh oregano plus sprigs for garnish or 1 teaspoon dried

½ teaspoon salt

½ teaspoon freshly ground pepper

1 medium zucchini (about 6 ounces), cut lengthwise into ½-inch slices

1 medium yellow summer squash (about 6 ounces), cut lengthwise into ½-inch slices

1 green bell pepper, seeded, quartered

1 yellow bell pepper, seeded, quartered

1 sweet onion, sliced ½-inch thick

2 tablespoons red wine vinegar

1 head romaine lettuce, torn into leaves

4 ounces crumbled feta cheese

Prepare a medium-hot charcoal fire or bring the grill to a medium-high heat.

In a small bowl, whisk together the oil, garlic, chopped mint and oregano, salt and pepper. Brush the cut sides of the vegetables with some of the mixture. Whisk the vinegar into the remaining oil mixture and reserve to use as a vinaigrette.

Grill the vegetables, turning once or twice, until lightly charred and softened, 6 to 8 minutes (the squash will take the least time).

Arrange the lettuce leaves on a platter or individual plates. Arrange the grilled vegetables on the lettuce. Drizzle with the reserved vinaigrette. Sprinkle with the cheese and garnish with the herb sprigs.

Spicy Vegetable Fritters

SERVES 6 TO 8

FRITTERS ARE ONE OF MY favorite comfort foods—crisp on the outside and soft and moist on the inside. They taste best right out of the pan but can be kept warm in a 200°F oven for a couple of hours. This recipe is versatile—it works well with most any vegetable. Try using it with any of your abundant garden harvests.

- 1 cup flour
- 1 cup whole wheat flour
- 1 teaspoon salt
- 1 teaspoon chili powder
- 1 teaspoon ground cumin
- 1 ¼ cups water
- 1 tablespoon lemon juice
- ½ pound shiitake mushrooms
- 1 small eggplant, sliced into rounds, then halved
- 2 zucchinis, cut into rounds
- ½ pound green beans, ends trimmed
- 4 green onions, chopped
- 1 onion, cut into rounds
- 1 sweet potato, cut into rounds
- 2 cups chopped tomatoes
- 1 red chili, seeded, chopped
- 1 garlic clove, crushed
- 1 onion, diced
- 1 tablespoon white wine vinegar
- 1 tablespoon brown sugar
- Salt and freshly ground pepper to taste
- Corn oil

Put the flours, salt, chili powder and cumin into a large bowl. Make a well in the middle and gradually add the water and lemon juice, beating until a smooth batter is formed.

Rinse the vegetables and allow them to dry completely. Put the tomatoes, red chili, garlic, diced onion, vinegar and brown sugar in the bowl of a food processor. Puree until smooth. Pour into a small saucepot and warm through over medium heat. Season with the salt and pepper and keep warm until the vegetables are ready.

Bring 4 inches of corn oil to 375°F in a deep pot over high heat. Working a few pieces at a time, dip the vegetables in the batter. Cover completely and hold each piece over the bowl to allow the excess to drip off. Drop the vegetables in the oil and fry until golden brown and the batter is puffy, about 2 to 5 minutes, depending on the vegetable. Remove with a slotted spoon to paper towels to drain and keep warm until all the vegetables are fried. Serve with small bowls of the sauce for dipping.

Curried Stir-Fry

SERVES 4 TO 6

"FUSION COOKING" IS THE combination of ingredients and cooking techniques from different cuisines around the world to create new, and even better flavors. Here I've combined traditional Indian curry with Japanese stir-fry and fresh American summer vegetables. It's important to have all your vegetables cut before you begin to stir-fry since they cook quickly.

¼	cup butter
1	shallot, minced
2	tablespoons curry powder
1	cup finely diced eggplant
2	tablespoons olive oil
1	cup peeled julienned sweet potato
4	small baby carrots, peeled, sliced
1	cup sliced zucchini
1	cup sliced yellow squash
1	cup 1-inch-cut snap beans
4	green onions (white and green parts), cut into 1-inch pieces
	Hot white rice
¼	cup minced fresh cilantro

Melt the butter in a large, heavy skillet over low heat. Add the shallot and sauté for 2 minutes. Stir in the curry powder and cook for another 2 minutes. Raise the heat to medium and add the eggplant. Stir frequently and brown on all sides, about 3 to 5 minutes. Add the olive oil as the eggplant absorbs the moisture. When the eggplant is lightly browned, add the sweet potato and carrots and sauté for 3 to 5 minutes. Stir in the zucchini and yellow squash and cook for another 3 to 5 minutes.

While the vegetables are cooking, bring a small pot of water to a boil. Add the beans and blanch for 2 minutes. Drain and add to the stir-fry along with the green onions. Toss well and when the green onions are bright green, about 2 to 4 minutes, remove from the heat.

Place hot white rice on each plate or in shallow bowls and top with the curried vegetables. Sprinkle with the cilantro and serve.

SIDES

Grilled Spiced Vegetables with
Dipping Sauce

Zucchini Salad

Matchstick Zucchini

Tomato, Corn and Red Onion Salad

Grilled Eggplant Italiano

Grilled Summer Vegetable Salad

Risotto-Style Corn

Grilled Asparagus with
Lemon Mayonnaise

Grilled Leeks

Southwestern Tomato Salad

Summer Squash and Onion Sauté

Minted Orzo Salad

Beer Batter Vidalia Onion Rings

Barley Bonanza

Seashore Fries

Moroccan Carrot Slaw

Grilled Potato Chips

Picnic Basket Potato Salad

Grilled Polenta and Tomatoes

Tabbouleh

Grilled Spiced Vegetables with Dipping Sauce

SERVES 4 TO 6

SUMMER SQUASH, BOTH THE YELLOW variety and its green sister, the zucchini, is one of my new favorite summertime staples. Grilling and then dipping them in this easy-to-make sauce is not only tasty, but also fun for the whole family.

1 tablespoon garlic powder

1 teaspoon freshly ground pepper

2 teaspoons ground coriander

½ teaspoon cayenne pepper

1 teaspoon ground cumin

½ eggplant, cut into ½-inch rounds

1 cup ½-inch bias-sliced yellow squash

1 cup ½-inch bias-sliced zucchini

1 portobello mushroom cap, cut into ½-inch slices

1 red onion, cut into 4 wedges

1 red bell pepper, halved, seeded

1 bunch green onions, roots trimmed

½ cup corn oil

½ cup pineapple juice

3 tablespoons corn oil

2 tablespoons brown sugar

1 teaspoon soy sauce

½ teaspoon freshly ground pepper

½ cup white vinegar

In a small bowl, combine the garlic powder, 1 teaspoon pepper, coriander, cayenne and cumin. Place all the vegetables in a large bowl. Sprinkle with the spice mixture and toss. Drizzle with the ½ cup corn oil and toss again. Place the vegetables on a grill over medium heat. Grill until browned on both sides and cooked through. Times will vary according to the vegetable.

Put the pineapple juice, 3 tablespoons corn oil, brown sugar, soy sauce, ½ teaspoon pepper and vinegar in a jar. Cover and shake well. When the brown sugar is dissolved, pour into small bowls and serve alongside the vegetables as a dipping sauce.

Matchstick Zucchini

THIS IS ONE GREAT SIDE DISH, for summer or any season. It takes a little extra work (and be sure you have a sharp knife!), but it's well worth it. It also makes a great base upon which you can place some grilled fish or chicken. There are any number of mandolin-type devices that will help you julienne the zucchini very quickly and easily. One other tip: try deep frying the matchsticks, then lightly salting them...you might never go back to potato chips.

2 medium zucchinis

2 tablespoons olive oil

2 garlic cloves, minced

½ teaspoon salt

Freshly ground pepper to taste

½ cup grated Parmesan cheese

Cut the zucchini into thin, lengthwise slices. Cut across the slices into thin, matchstick pieces.

Heat the oil in a medium-size skillet over medium heat. Add the garlic and zucchini and cook, stirring gently, for 2 to 3 minutes. Sprinkle with the salt, pepper and Parmesan cheese, toss and serve.

Grilled Eggplant Italiano

SERVES 4 TO 6

I RECENTLY LEARNED SOMETHING ABOUT EGGPLANTS. They are really a fruit, a member of the berry family. To cut down on the bitter taste, try slicing and then salting them. Let them rest for about half an hour and then pat them dry with a paper towel before tossing on the oil and spices.

1 large eggplant, cut into ½-inch slices
¾ cup olive oil
2 teaspoons garlic powder
1 teaspoon salt
1 teaspoon oregano
¼ cup minced fresh parsley
¼ cup minced fresh basil

Brush the eggplant rounds with some of the olive oil. Sprinkle with the garlic powder, salt and oregano. Place on a grill over medium heat and cook 3 to 4 minutes until browned. Turn them and brown on the other side. Remove to a platter and sprinkle with the fresh herbs. Drizzle with the remaining olive oil.

Risotto-Style Corn

SERVES 4 TO 6

RUN, DON'T WALK, TO THE NEAREST FARMSTAND when you start to see fresh corn on the cob for sale! It is one of summertime's best treats. And this recipe takes this quintessential American crop and adds a traditional Italian preparation technique usually reserved for rice to create a new and wonderful variation on creamed corn.

2	tablespoons unsalted butter
1	large red onion, chopped
1	red bell pepper, seeded, chopped
2	cups fresh corn kernels
1	tablespoon chopped fresh sage
¾	cup chicken stock
1	cup heavy cream
1	teaspoon salt

Melt the butter in a large skillet over medium heat. Add the onion and red pepper and sauté for 5 minutes, stirring often. Add the corn, sage and chicken stock and bring to a boil. Stir constantly and simmer for 7 minutes. Add the cream and salt. Continue to cook and stir for another 7 minutes. Transfer to a warm serving bowl and serve.

Grilled Leeks

THE MOST IMPORTANT THING to remember about cooking with leeks is to make sure they are thoroughly washed since they often contain a lot of grit. It's best to slice them first and then toss them in a colander and rinse several times under running water.

4   ¾-inch-diameter leeks

2   tablespoons olive oil

1   tablespoon chopped fresh thyme plus sprigs for garnish or 1 teaspoon dried thyme

Salt and freshly ground pepper to taste

Prepare a medium-hot charcoal fire or bring the grill to a medium-high heat. Trim the leeks to include 1 inch of the pale green parts. Wash and dry the leeks. In a small dish, combine the oil, thyme, salt and pepper to taste.

Grill the leeks, turning often, until softened and golden brown, 6 to 8 minutes. Garnish with the thyme sprigs and serve.

Summer Squash and Onion Sauté

SERVES 4

CREAMED VEGETABLES ARE ONE OF those decadent indulgences I just love. But in this dish, I use just a little bit of sour cream to combine with the sweet caramelized onions and squash for a healthier creamed dish. By the way, the fennel fronds called for in this recipe are those little, green, dill-looking growths at the top of a fennel bulb.

2 tablespoons olive oil

3 small yellow squash, trimmed, cut into ¼-inch slices

1 small onion, sliced

2 tablespoons minced fennel fronds

1 tablespoon chopped fresh oregano

¼ cup sour cream

½ teaspoon salt

¼ teaspoon freshly ground pepper

1 tablespoon minced fresh chives

Heat the oil in a large skillet over medium heat. Add the squash and onion and toss to coat with the oil. Cover, lower the heat to low and cook for 6 minutes. Stir in the fennel, oregano and sour cream. Season with the salt and pepper and just heat through. Sprinkle with the chives and serve.

Beer Batter Vidalia Onion Rings

SERVES 4

I FIRST TASTED A VIDALIA AS A KID. I had walked into the kitchen and found my dad eating an onion like an apple. I was astonished, and thought he was crazy...until he coaxed me into taking a bite. Since then, the months of May and June—when the sweet and juicy Vidalias from Georgia first become available—have been kind of special to me. Luckily, Vidalias are available in most parts of the country year 'round now, so you can enjoy them whenever you get the urge. The beer batter used here is something my dad came up with for my sister Mag... she loved onion rings. So while Dad and I crunched them raw, Mag enjoyed hers deep fried. You can take your pick.

1 cup plus 2 tablespoons flour

1 teaspoon salt

½ teaspoon freshly ground black pepper

½ teaspoon white pepper

⅛ teaspoon cayenne pepper

1 cup beer

1 quart corn oil

1 large (at least 1 pound) Vidalia onion, cut into ½-inch slices, separated into rings

Coarse salt

Combine the flour, salt and peppers in a large mixing bowl. Add the beer and whisk until smooth. Cover and set aside for 30 minutes.

In a large pot fitted with a fryer basket, bring the corn oil to 350°F. Stir the batter. It should be thicker than pancake batter, but if it is too thick, add more beer. Dip the onion rings in the batter to completely coat. Allow the excess to drip back into the bowl and place in the oil. Fry 3 or 4 rings at a time for 2 to 3 minutes, until golden brown. Drain on paper towels and keep warm in the oven until all the onions are fried. Sprinkle the cooked onions with the coarse salt and serve immediately.

Seashore Fries

SERVES 4

EVERY SUMMER WHEN I WAS A KID, we went to Avalon, New Jersey, and the first stop we made was to a small shop at the end of the boardwalk where they made these fries. I have never come across their equal, though there are several chains now that claim they make the best "board-walk fries." I won't debate whether they do or they don't, but this is the recipe I grew up with in Avalon, and I'm always of the mind that the best you can do is go to the source.

4 large potatoes, peeled, cut into ¼-inch-thick long strips

2 quarts corn oil

Coarse salt

White vinegar

Place the cut potatoes in a medium-size bowl of warm water to rinse off excess starch. Lift out of the water and dry very well with paper towels.

In a deep pot fitted with a fryer basket, bring the corn oil to 350°F. Drop the potatoes, a handful at a time, into the oil. Fry for 5 to 7 minutes, until they are golden brown, and then remove from the oil. Drain on paper towels, sprinkle with the salt and keep warm until all the potatoes are cooked.

Layer 2 sheets of newspaper on a flat surface. Roll from one corner, making it into a cone. Fold the bottom of the cone so nothing will fall out. Fold 4 cones.

Fill the cones with the fries and sprinkle with the vinegar. Serve immediately.

Grilled Potato Chips

MY DAUGHTER TAYLOR LOVES these. And I like them because Taylor's not getting a lot of fat and calories from them since they're grilled, not deep fried. And they're so easy to make! While we want the grill to be very hot for most recipes, for this one medium is best, or move the grate away from the coals. If the potatoes get too close to the fire, they will burn. The key is to keep turning them until they are cooked through and crispy. Try using a fish fillet barbecue basket.

2 large baking potatoes (about 1 pound total)

3 to 4 tablespoons olive oil

Salt and freshly ground pepper to taste

Prepare a medium-hot charcoal fire or bring the grill to a medium heat. Cut the unpeeled potatoes into lengthwise slices about ½-inch thick. Brush both sides of each slice with the oil, then sprinkle them lightly with the salt and pepper.

Grill the potatoes, turning occasionally with a side spatula, until crisp and browned, 10 to 14 minutes. Sprinkle with additional salt and pepper.

Grilled Polenta and Tomatoes

SERVES 4

I love polenta. Period. I never had it, though, until it started popping up in restaurants as a side dish—the new "in" thing a few years back. Now you can buy ready-made polenta, which makes this recipe much easier to handle. Tossing it on the grill gives it a great crust and makes it perfect as a base for those beef-steak tomatoes.

5 tablespoons olive oil

2 garlic cloves, chopped

1 tablespoon chopped fresh basil plus ¾ cup basil leaves

1 10- to 12-ounce prepared polenta roll, sliced crosswise ½-inch thick

2 meaty tomatoes, sliced ½-inch thick

   Salt and freshly ground pepper to taste

1 tablespoon balsamic vinegar

Prepare a medium-hot charcoal fire or bring the grill to a medium-high heat. In a small dish, stir together the oil, garlic and chopped basil. Brush both sides of the polenta and tomato slices with some of the flavored oil, then sprinkle with the salt and pepper.

Grill the polenta and tomatoes, turning once, until softened and grill marks appear, about 8 minutes for the polenta and 2 to 3 minutes for the tomatoes.

Arrange the polenta and tomato slices on plates or a platter, interspersed with the basil leaves. Whisk the vinegar into the remaining oil mixture, then drizzle over the polenta and tomatoes.

Zucchini Salad

THIS IS A GREAT WAY TO MAKE a change from the standard lettuce and tomato salad. It has a deeper, richer flavor to it as well. A food processor makes easy work of the shredding, and is a real timesaver. And it's a great way to get the kids to eat some veggies—when they don't look like veggies, the kids will go on taste, and this salad has a lot of that.

- 2 medium zucchinis, trimmed, halved lengthwise
- ½ red bell pepper, seeded
- 1 teaspoon Dijon-style mustard
- ¼ teaspoon salt
- ½ teaspoon freshly ground pepper
- ½ teaspoon herbes de Provence
- 2 tablespoons red wine vinegar
- ⅓ cup extra-virgin olive oil
- 1 medium tomato, cut in eighths

Fit a food processor with a shredding blade and push the zucchini and red pepper through the feeding tube. Place the mixture in a colander and allow to drain as you make the dressing. In a small bowl, whisk together the mustard, salt, pepper, herbes de Provence and vinegar. Slowly add the olive oil, whisking constantly. Place the zucchini, red pepper and tomato in a serving bowl and toss with the dressing.

Tomato, Corn and Red Onion Salad

SERVES 4

MY FATHER'S SIDE OF THE FAMILY talked fondly of Silver Queen corn, a variety which was trucked from the Eastern Shore of Maryland. It was one of the first sweet corns I tasted. One bite and you'll know why it remains a family favorite even today. If you can't find Silver Queen, then just select the sweetest corn available.

½ teaspoon freshly ground pepper

½ teaspoon coarse salt

2 tablespoons fresh thyme leaves or 2 teaspoons dried

2 tablespoons balsamic vinegar

¼ cup extra-virgin olive oil

1 ear white corn on the cob (such as Silver Queen)

3 large tomatoes, thinly sliced

¼ red onion, cut into paper-thin slices

½ jalapeño pepper, seeded, minced

Place the pepper, salt, thyme leaves and balsamic vinegar in a small bowl. Using a wire whisk, slowly add the olive oil.

Bring a small pot of water to a boil. Working over the bowl used for the vinaigrette to catch any sweet juices, cut the corn off the cob. Lift the kernels out with a slotted spoon and place in the pot of boiling water. Cook for 2 to 3 minutes, drain and rinse with cool water. Set aside on a paper towel to dry.

Arrange the tomato and onion slices on a serving platter. Sprinkle with the corn kernels and jalapeño peppers. Spoon the vinaigrette over the salad and serve.

Grilled Summer Vegetable Salad

SERVES 4 TO 6

My cousin, Tim Wilson, is the first guy who turned me on to grilling all kinds of vegetables. He's a master griller—even smokes his own meats—and until I spent some time barbecuing with him, I'd really not considered how sweet and flavorful vegetables become when grilled. As for the salad, adding grilled vegetables is a great change from grilled chicken or beef, and makes a much lower-fat dish for those watching their weight. It's also versatile, in that you can pretty much use any vegetables that are in season.

2 tablespoons red wine vinegar

¼ teaspoon salt

½ teaspoon freshly ground pepper

1 tablespoon chopped fresh marjoram or 1 teaspoon dried

1 garlic clove, minced

⅓ cup olive oil

½ red bell pepper, seeded

½ green bell pepper, seeded

4 button mushrooms

4 green onions, roots trimmed

1 ear corn on the cob, husked

1 small head romaine lettuce, rinsed, cut into bite-size pieces

Put the vinegar, salt, pepper, marjoram and garlic in a small bowl. Using a wire whisk, slowly add the olive oil. Set aside.

Grill the peppers, mushrooms, green onions and corn on the cob, turning as they brown, over medium heat. The peppers, mushrooms and green onions will take about 4 minutes to cook and the corn 8 to 10 minutes. When cool enough to handle, cut the peppers into thin strips, quarter the mushrooms, cut the green onions into 1-inch pieces and cut the corn kernels off the cob. Place them in a small bowl, and toss with half of the vinaigrette and refrigerate.

When the grilled vegetables are chilled, place the romaine in a salad bowl and toss with the remaining vinaigrette. Sprinkle the grilled vegetables on top of the salad and serve.

Grilled Asparagus with Lemon Mayonnaise

SERVES 4

I LIKE TO USE ONE OF THOSE grill baskets or hinged racks to grill my asparagus to assure they don't wind up in the coals. But for larger spears it's just as easy to lay them crosswise on the grates and rotate to make sure they are cooked through. These are a favorite at my backyard barbecues and make an unusual accompaniment to burgers.

1 lemon

6 tablespoons mayonnaise

1 pound fresh asparagus, tough stalk ends snapped off

2 tablespoons olive or vegetable oil

Grate 1 teaspoon of peel from the lemon and squeeze 1 tablespoon of juice. Mix the lemon peel and juice with the mayonnaise. Refrigerate for at least 15 minutes or up to 6 hours.

Prepare a medium-hot charcoal fire or bring the grill to a medium-high heat. Brush the asparagus spears with the oil. Lay the spears crosswise on the grill so they don't fall through. Grill, turning often with tongs, until softened and lightly browned, 8 to 11 minutes depending upon the thickness of the spears.

Arrange the asparagus on a serving platter. Spoon a ribbon of mayonnaise over the center of the spears.

Southwestern Tomato Salad

I LOVE MY FOOD HOT AND often have a problem finding a great salad recipe that provides that extra kick. Combining jalapeño peppers with ripe, summertime tomatoes is a quick and easy way to get a bit of that Southwestern flavor all season long.

3 large ripe tomatoes, thinly sliced

1 small jalapeño pepper, seeded, minced

2 tablespoons minced green onions

1 green bell pepper, seeded, julienned

2 tablespoons extra-virgin olive oil

1 tablespoon red wine vinegar

Salt and freshly ground pepper to taste

Arrange the tomatoes, overlapping, on a serving dish. In a medium-size bowl, mix together the remaining ingredients and spoon over the tomatoes.

Minted Orzo Salad

MY WIFE TONI'S RICH ITALIAN HERITAGE has brought a love of pasta to our family. And orzo is one of her favorites. It is one of the smallest pastas and is shaped like rice, making it ideal for warm weather salads. This recipe brings not only the best of Italy to your table, but you'll find some other great Mediterranean touches in it as well.

1 pound orzo

1 tablespoon salt

½ red bell pepper, seeded, diced

¼ cup diced red onion

½ cup chopped fresh mint

⅓ cup crumbled Gorgonzola cheese

2 carrots, peeled, diced

½ cup fresh peas

⅓ cup olive oil

½ cup pine nuts

1 cucumber, peeled, seeded, diced

Salt and freshly ground pepper to taste

Cook the orzo in salted water as directed on the package. Drain, place in a large mixing bowl and immediately mix in the red pepper, onion, mint and crumbled cheese. Set aside.

In a small pot of boiling water, blanch the carrots for 2 minutes. Add the peas and cook for another 2 minutes. Drain and fold into the orzo. Drizzle the olive oil over the salad and toss to coat. Cover and refrigerate until cold.

In a small, heavy skillet over medium heat, sauté the pine nuts, stirring often, until they begin to brown, about 3 to 5 minutes. Remove them immediately from the pan and set aside.

Just before serving, fold in the cucumber. Adjust the seasoning with salt and pepper and sprinkle with the pine nuts.

Barley Bonanza

SERVES 8

GRAINS ARE MAKING A BIG COMEBACK on menus and for good reason. They are good for us and add great texture to dishes while supplying a rich and natural source of vitamins and protein. This side dish can easily be converted into a hearty main course by adding shrimp, chicken or even tofu.

1	cup barley, rinsed
½	teaspoon salt
2	ears bicolor corn on the cob
¼	cup diced red onion
¼	cup chopped fresh basil
2	green onions, minced
1	red bell pepper, seeded, diced
1	cup ½-inch-cut green beans
½	cup fresh peas
3	tablespoons red wine vinegar
1	teaspoon fresh lemon juice
1	tablespoon Dijon-style mustard
½	teaspoon salt
½	teaspoon freshly ground pepper
1	teaspoon ground cumin
½	cup olive oil

Bring the barley to a boil in 5 cups of cold water in a large pot. Add the salt, reduce the heat to a simmer, cover and cook for 1¼ hours. Pour into a fine-meshed strainer to drain off any excess water and place in a large mixing bowl. Cut the corn kernels from the cob. Fold in the corn, onion, basil, green onions and red pepper and set aside.

Blanch the green beans in boiling water for 4 minutes. Add the peas and boil for another 2 minutes. Drain and stir into the barley mixture.

In a small mixing bowl, whisk together the vinegar, lemon juice, mustard, salt, pepper and cumin. Slowly add the olive oil.

Toss the barley salad with the vinaigrette. Cover and refrigerate until chilled. Serve cold or at room temperature.

Moroccan Carrot Slaw

One of my friends recently came back from Morocco and wouldn't stop talking about the fantastic vegetable salads that are served—sometimes as many as ten different dishes make up the salad course. Carrots combined with cumin is one dish visitors to Morocco often bring back home to duplicate.

½ pound carrots, peeled, finely grated

½ cup raisins

½ cup pine nuts

1 teaspoon Dijon-style mustard

2 teaspoons red wine vinegar

1 garlic clove, minced

½ teaspoon ground cumin

½ teaspoon freshly ground pepper

1 teaspoon salt

¾ cup olive oil

Place the carrots and raisins in a large bowl and toss well. In a small, heavy skillet over medium heat, sauté the pine nuts until they just begin to brown. Remove immediately to the carrots and raisins and toss well.

In a small bowl, combine the mustard, vinegar, garlic, cumin, pepper and salt. Using a wire whisk, slowly add the oil to form an emulsion. Pour the vinaigrette over the slaw and toss until it is well coated.

Picnic Basket Potato Salad

SERVES 4 TO 6

I LOVE TO EAT OUTDOORS and what's a backyard barbeque without potato salad? This recipe is ideal for picnics or potlucks since it doesn't contain mayonnaise, which doesn't fare well with summer's temperatures. Still it's important to refrigerate this salad for at least a half hour to assure that all the flavors combine.

- 1 pound new potatoes
- 1 tablespoon salt
- 2 tablespoons cider vinegar
- 2 teaspoons Dijon-style mustard
- 1 tablespoon chopped fresh marjoram or 1 teaspoon dried
- ½ teaspoon freshly ground pepper
- ½ teaspoon salt
- ½ cup extra-virgin olive oil
- ½ red bell pepper, seeded, diced
- 3 green onions, trimmed, finely chopped

Wash and cut the potatoes into 1-inch pieces. Place in a medium-size pot and cover with cold water. Add the 1 tablespoon salt and bring to a boil. Lower the heat until the water simmers and cook for 7 to 10 minutes, until a sample potato slips from a fork when speared.

While the potatoes are cooking, make the vinaigrette. In a small bowl, combine the vinegar, mustard, marjoram, pepper and ½ teaspoon salt. Using a wire whisk, slowly add the oil to form an emulsion.

Drain the potatoes and place in a large bowl along with the bell pepper and green onions. Pour the vinaigrette over the potatoes and toss well. Cover and refrigerate for 30 minutes. Toss gently just before serving.

Tabbouleh

SERVES 4 TO 6

THIS DISH IS A CLASSIC MIDDLE EAST favorite that tastes best when served at room temperature. To eat the salad, scoop out a helping with endive leaves as the recipe suggests or toss some pita bread in a toaster and serve warm. Allow guests to rip off a piece or cut the pita bread into triangles for easier handling.

1 cup bulgur wheat

½ cup fresh lemon juice

1 bunch green onions

1 cup chopped fresh parsley

1 cup chopped fresh mint

3 tomatoes, seeded, chopped

⅓ cup extra-virgin olive oil

1 teaspoon salt

½ teaspoon freshly cracked pepper

12 endive leaves

Place the bulgur in a medium bowl and cover with warm water. Cover and let stand for 1 hour. Drain in a fine sieve. Return to the bowl and fold in the lemon juice, green onions, parsley, mint and tomatoes. Let stand for another 30 minutes. Stir well and fold in the olive oil, salt and pepper.

Place the tabbouleh in a serving bowl and surround with the endive leaves.

DESSERTS

White Peach Tart

Blueberry and Almond Galette

Lemon Mousse

Grilled Georgia Peaches à la Mode

Raspberry Fool

Strawberry-Rhubarb Pie

Summer Berry Pudding

Frozen Raspberry Soufflé

Fourth of July Ice Cream Cake

Fresh Mint Chocolate Chip Ice Cream

Fresh Berry Shortcake

Grilled-Lemon-Sesame Bananas

Soused Peaches

Berry Patch Popsicles

Upside-Down Cherries and Berries Cake

White Russian Berries

Warm Summer Berries on Sorbet

White Peach Tart

SERVES 8

WHEN MY FAMILY FIRST MOVED TO Delaware, our new house was right on the edge of a peach orchard. Every summer, my sister, brother, and I would jump the fence and grab fresh peaches hanging low on the branches of the trees. They were incredible! My dad, by that time, was deep into his baking phase, so this tart was inevitable. White peaches are best, but any peach will do.

1¼ cups flour

1 tablespoon plus 1 teaspoon sugar

1 teaspoon vanilla extract

½ cup unsalted butter, chilled, cut into small dice

1 egg yolk, beaten

1 to 2 tablespoons ice water

6 white-fleshed slightly firm peaches

1 cup dry white wine

2 tablespoons honey

4 whole cloves

8 ounces apricot or peach preserves

2 tablespoons water

Put the flour and sugar in the bowl of a food processor. With the motor running, add the vanilla and butter, a few pieces at a time. Add the egg yolk and then the ice water, a little at a time, until the dough just holds together. Place the dough on a sheet of plastic wrap and press into a circular disc. Cover with the wrap and chill for 1 hour.

Preheat the oven to 400°F. Roll the dough out on a lightly floured surface to a 12-inch circle. Lift the dough into a 10-inch tart pan with a removable bottom. Gently press the dough into the corners and up the sides. Trim the edges with a sharp knife. Cover the filled pan with aluminum foil and weigh down the bottom with some dry beans. Bake for 15 to 18 minutes. Remove the foil and bake for another 3 to 5 minutes, until it is dry and golden brown. Remove to a rack and allow to cool completely.

Place the peaches in a deep pot of boiling water. Poach for 30 seconds. Drain and run under cold water. Peel off the skins, halve and remove the pits. Cut into ½-inch slices. Bring the wine, honey and cloves to a boil in a large skillet. Scatter the peach slices on the bottom and gently stir to coat. Cover and simmer for 5 minutes. Lift the slices out of the poaching liquid with a slotted spoon and arrange in the tart shell in a circular, shingled fashion.

Melt the preserves in a small saucepot over high heat. Add the water to thin it out slightly and remove from the heat to cool down. Brush the peach slices with the glaze and place in a cool spot for 30 minutes. Remove the tart from its pan and serve.

Blueberry and Almond Galette

SERVES 8

As the former partner in a restaurant, I can tell you that the biggest secret of most pastry chefs is that they use frozen puff pastry. It's usually available near the ice cream in your local grocery and can be easily thawed in about a half hour before using. This galette is a great recipe for the kids to try out since it looks and tastes like a sweet-dough, fruit pizza.

6 ounces slivered almonds

1 8 x 10-inch pre-made puff pastry sheet (thawed if frozen)

2 pints blueberries

3 tablespoons sugar

4 tablespoons unsalted butter, cut into small cubes

Preheat the oven to 375°F. Place the almonds in a food processor and pulse until well ground. Spread on a baking sheet and toast until light brown, about 10 minutes. Remove from the oven and set aside.

Cover a baking sheet with parchment paper. Place the puff pastry on the parchment. Brush the edges with water and fold over to form a border. Spread the blueberries over the puff pastry and sprinkle with the ground almonds and sugar. Dot with the butter.

Bake the galette at 375°F for 45 minutes to 1 hour, until it is crisp and bubbling. Cool on a metal rack and cut into 8 squares to serve.

Lemon Mousse

WE STILL LIKE TO CALL MY BROTHER PAUL the "Dessert Master" because for a time he turned his talents into a business supplying sweet concoctions to top restaurants in the Denver area. This is one of those recipes I know he would love because it looks and tastes like something one of those four-star restaurants would serve but is actually a fairly simple stovetop creation that can be made in less than 15 minutes.

4 egg yolks

½ cup sugar

⅓ cup fresh lemon juice

2 teaspoons lemon zest

1 cup heavy cream

½ pint raspberries

Mint leaves for garnish

In the top of a double boiler, combine the egg yolks, sugar, lemon juice and zest. Using a wire whisk, slowly cook the lemon curd over gently simmering water until it becomes slightly thick, about 4 minutes. Remove from the heat and let cool.

Place the heavy cream in another bowl and beat with a whisk or an electric beater until it forms soft peaks. Fold ¾ of the cream into the cooled lemon mixture.

Drop the raspberries in the bottom of 4 glass goblets and pour the mousse on top. Use the remaining cream as dollops on the top of the mousse. Refrigerate for 30 minutes. Garnish with a sprig of mint and serve.

Grilled Georgia Peaches à la Mode

SERVES 4

OF COURSE, THE PEACHES DON'T have to be from Georgia but if you can find them, you've got to try them grilled. Otherwise, use any firm peaches—or even firm pears, nectarines or apricots for that matter. Be sure to drizzle plenty of the sauce over the ice cream. Nothing goes better together than warm fruit and ice cream.

- 2 tablespoons unsalted butter
- 5 tablespoons honey
- 1½ tablespoons lemon juice
- 2 tablespoons Cognac, brandy or orange juice
- 4 ripe but firm peaches, peeled, halved, pitted
- 8 small scoops vanilla ice cream
- ¼ cup chopped pistachio nuts or toasted pecans

Prepare a medium charcoal fire or bring the grill to a medium heat. In a small saucepan, melt the butter with the honey over low heat. Stir in the lemon juice and Cognac. Brush the peaches all over with the sauce.

Grill, turning once with a spatula, just until the peaches begin to soften and grill marks appear, 2 to 3 minutes total.

Serve the peach halves topped with small scoops of ice cream. Sprinkle with the nuts and drizzle with any remaining syrup.

Raspberry Fool

A FOOL IS JUST ABOUT ONE of the simplest desserts you can make. I know from experience. Just fold pureed fruit into whipped cream and serve. While I prefer raspberries—especially when they are at their peak in June—any other summer-time berry could be made a fool of as well.

1 tablespoon sugar

1 pint raspberries, mashed

1 cup very cold heavy cream

1 teaspoon vanilla extract

½ pint raspberries

Stir the sugar into the mashed raspberries set in a large bowl.

Beat the cream and vanilla extract in a chilled bowl with an electric mixer until soft peaks are formed. Scrape into the bowl with the raspberries and gently fold until the mixture is well blended. Spoon into glass goblets, drop a few whole raspberries on the top of each fool and serve.

Strawberry-Rhubarb Pie

SERVES 8 TO 10

THERE IS NO OTHER DESSERT THAT reminds me more of the great Midwest than those made from rhubarb. A visit to my family in the nation's heartland invariably includes at least one meal finished off with rhubarb pie. Combining this tart fruit with sweet strawberries makes an even greater pie that I plan to make the next time I'm visiting—I hope it becomes a family classic.

2 cups hulled quartered strawberries

3 cups sliced rhubarb

1¼ cups sugar

¼ cup quick-cooking tapioca

1 tablespoon lemon juice

¼ teaspoon salt

⅛ teaspoon ground cloves

2 9-inch frozen pie crusts, thawed

Preheat the oven to 425°F. Place the strawberries and rhubarb in a large bowl. Combine the sugar, tapioca, lemon juice, salt and ground cloves in a small bowl. Pour the mixture over the fruit and toss to mix well. Let sit for 15 minutes.

While the filling is resting, turn one of the pie crusts onto a lightly floured board. Gently roll out the dough, working from the center out until it is an inch wider than the pie pan. Using a knife or a decorative pastry wheel, cut the dough into ½-inch strips. Pour the filling into the second pie shell and begin to weave the top.

Place 5 to 7 strips across the pie. Weave a cross strip through the center of the pie by folding back every other strip going the other way. Continue weaving in this way, folding alternate cross strips back each time a new strip is added. Trim off the overhanging ends. Using wet fingers to help form a seal, pinch together the bottom shell and the lattice top. Bake the pie for 45 minutes.

Desserts

Summer Berry Pudding

CRÈME FRAÎCHE IS ONE OF THOSE ingredients I have come to love. Crème fraîche is a mature, thickened cream very popular in France. While it is sold as a gourmet—and thus pricey—item in America, you can make your own for only pennies. Combine one cup of whipping cream and two tablespoons of buttermilk in a glass container. Cover and let stand at room temperature for eight to 24 hours and you have crème fraîche.

1 cup ricotta cheese

1 cup crème fraîche or sour cream

⅓ cup sugar

1 pint raspberries

1 tablespoon fresh lemon juice

1 pint blackberries

Place the ricotta, crème fraîche and sugar in the bowl of a food processor. Pulse until smooth. Scrape down once or twice. With the motor running, add the raspberries and lemon juice and process until smooth.

Scoop the pudding into a large mixing bowl and gently fold in the blackberries. Spoon the pudding into glass goblets and refrigerate for 1 hour before serving.

Frozen Raspberry Soufflé

SERVES 6 TO 8

WHAT'S GREAT ABOUT THIS SOUFFLÉ is that you don't have to worry about it falling since it is frozen. This dessert makes a great presentation when served right from the soufflé dish with the waxed paper collar removed. I like to put plenty of spoons centrally located on the table to allow friends to dig in and eat right from the soufflé dish. No extra bowls have to be dirtied.

2 tablespoons unflavored gelatin

1 cup sugar

Pinch salt

3 cups raspberries

½ cup lemon juice

6 large eggs, separated

¼ teaspoon almond extract

Confectioner's sugar

Stir together the gelatin, ½ cup of the sugar and the salt in a small saucepot. Puree the raspberries and lemon juice in a blender or food processor, until smooth.

In a small mixing bowl, lightly beat the egg yolks. Mix in 1 cup of the raspberry puree. Stir the mixture into the saucepot. Let bloom for 5 minutes. Cook over low heat for about 5 minutes, until the gelatin is dissolved. Remove from the heat and stir in the remaining puree and the almond extract. Chill, stirring occasionally, until the mixture is pudding-like.

Beat the egg whites with an electric mixer on high speed until soft peaks form, about 5 minutes. Gradually add the remaining ½ cup of sugar and continue beating until stiff, but not dry, peaks form. Pour the puree into a large mixing bowl. Add the egg whites and gently fold until well combined.

Wrap a double layer of waxed paper around a 1½-quart soufflé dish and secure with string. Be sure that the collar is at least 3 inches above the top rim of the dish. Pour the soufflé into the dish. Smooth the top and freeze for 4 hours.

Just before serving, remove the collar. Dust with the confectioner's sugar and spoon into glass goblets.

Fourth of July Ice Cream Cake

SERVES 8

MY NEIGHBORS REFER TO THIS dessert as "Red-White-and-Blue Cake" since each layer of ice cream is a different patriotic color. It does make the perfect Fourth of July dessert but really gets the family in the summertime mood when served at Memorial Day—or any warm day for that matter.

3 cups vanilla ice cream, softened

1 loaf pound cake

1 pint blueberries

1 pint raspberries

Line a 9 x 5-inch loaf pan with enough plastic wrap to allow for at least 4 inches of overhang on each side of the pan.

Scoop 1 cup of the ice cream and the blueberries into the bowl of an electric mixer fitted with a paddle. Working on low speed, mix until the berries are incorporated. Using a rubber spatula, scrape the mixture into the loaf pan and spread it evenly across the bottom. Bang the pan on a counter several times to make sure the ice cream is completely filling the pan.

Place the pound cake on its side and cut lengthwise into 1-inch-thick slices. Place the slices on a baking sheet and toast until lightly browned, under the broiler, about 2 to 4 minutes. Turn and toast the other side. Place 1 slice of toasted pound cake on top of the blueberry ice cream. If the cake does not completely cover the ice cream, use 1 slice and cut off enough cake to fill in the gap.

Spread 1 cup of plain vanilla ice cream on top and then add another layer of cake.

Clean out the mixing bowl and then add the remaining ice cream and raspberries. Mix on low speed with a paddle until blended. Spread the mixture on the top layer of cake.

Cover the pan with plastic wrap and freeze for at least 2 hours. Just before serving, remove the covering wrap. Dip the pan in a deep bowl of hot water for 20 seconds. Remove and holding the excess plastic wrap, lift the cake out of the pan. Flip over onto a serving platter and remove the remaining plastic. Cut into 1-inch pieces to serve.

Fresh Mint Chocolate Chip Ice Cream

SERVES 4

HERE'S A GREAT TRICK TO CREATE a homemade, flavored ice cream without spending much time, effort or expense. I like to add some of my favorite ingredients—including bits of chocolate—to already frozen vanilla ice cream. The results outdo most store-bought varieties and can be made way ahead.

4 ounces semisweet chocolate

1 pint vanilla ice cream, softened

4 drops peppermint extract

⅓ cup minced fresh mint

Coarsely chop the chocolate and set aside.

Scoop the ice cream into the bowl of an electric mixer fitted with a paddle. Working on slow speed, add the drops of peppermint, fresh mint and finally the chocolate. Mix until all the ingredients are evenly distributed. Scrape into a smaller bowl, cover and freeze for 2 hours before serving.

Fresh Berry Shortcake

SERVES 6

WHY SERVE YOUR GUESTS THOSE store-bought sponge cakes when you can make your own shortcakes using a muffin mold faster than it takes to get in and out of the store. While the recipe calls for superfine sugar which can be found at many specialty stores, simply mix regular granulated sugar in the food processor for a couple of minutes and you will have made your own superfine sugar.

½ cup cake flour

⅛ teaspoon salt

3 eggs, separated

½ cup superfine sugar

2 teaspoons lemon juice

½ teaspoon lemon zest

3 cups berries (such as blueberries, raspberries or hulled, quartered strawberries)

¼ cup sugar

1 cup heavy cream

2 tablespoons sour cream

1 teaspoon vanilla extract

Preheat the oven to 350°F. Line 6 muffin molds with paper liners. In a small bowl, combine the flour and salt. In another small bowl, using a wire whisk, beat the egg yolks until thick and lemon colored. Clean the whisk with soap and warm water and beat the egg whites in a large, very clean bowl until stiff but not dry. Add the superfine sugar, 2 tablespoons at a time, to the egg whites, beating well. Beat in the lemon juice and zest. Fold the yolks into the whites gently. Fold in the flour mixture slowly. Continue folding for about 2 minutes to blend well. Fill the muffin cups about half full. Bake for 18 minutes or until a toothpick inserted into a sample cupcake comes out clean. Remove to a wire rack to cool.

In a medium-size bowl, toss the berries with the sugar and set aside for 30 minutes. Using a wire whisk or an electric mixer, combine the heavy cream, sour cream and vanilla extract. Beat until it forms soft peaks. To assemble, remove the paper from the cupcakes and hollow out the center, about the size of a ping-pong ball. Fill with whipped cream and mound over the top of each cupcake. Spoon the berries and some of their syrup over the top.

Grilled Lemon-Sesame Bananas

SERVES 4

USING THE GRILL TO MAKE DESSERT is a great way to keep the heat out of the kitchen during the hot months. The key to creating the perfect grilled banana is to make sure that the grill is at a medium heat. The banana should start to sizzle as soon as it hits the grill. If it doesn't, remove it immediately and allow the grill to heat up more.

1 lemon

¼ cup pure maple syrup

2 tablespoons unsalted butter

4 ripe but firm bananas, peeled, halved lengthwise

1½ tablespoons sesame seeds

4 mint sprigs for garnish

Prepare a medium to charcoal fire or bring the grill to a medium heat. Grate 1 teaspoon of peel from the lemon and squeeze 1 tablespoon of juice. In a small saucepan, heat together the lemon juice, peel, maple syrup and butter just until the butter melts.

Brush or dip the banana halves into the maple lemon mixture. Then sprinkle or roll in the sesame seeds to coat lightly.

Grill the bananas, turning once or twice with a spatula, until the fruit is lightly browned and softened, but not mushy, and the seeds are toasted, 3 to 5 minutes. Serve garnished with the mint sprigs.

Soused Peaches

THERE IS NO BETTER WAY TO get your peaches a bit tipsy than by using grappa, an Italian after-dinner drink made from the grape skins and seeds left in a wine press. You should be able to find it at your local liquor store. If you can't find grappa, try marinating the peaches in Port instead.

1 cup grappa (Italian *eau de vie*)

2 tablespoons minced fresh mint

4 ripe peaches

Mint sprigs for garnish

Bring the grappa and minced mint to a boil in a small pot. Cover, remove from the heat and let steep for 20 minutes.

Bring a deep pot of water to a boil. Add the peaches and blanch for 30 seconds. Drain and rinse under cold water. Remove the skins, halve and remove the pits. Slice each peach into ½-inch slices and place in a medium-size bowl. Strain the grappa mixture over the peaches. Toss and set aside for 2 hours, stirring occasionally.

Garnish with a sprig of fresh mint and serve the marinated peaches over ice cream, pound cake or with a dollop of crème fraîche.

Berry Patch Popsicles

MAKES 6 POPSICLES

POPSICLES HAVE TO BE A KID'S BEST friend in summertime. But I don't like my daughter Taylor to eat all the sugar that's in most popsicles available in the grocery freezer. Here's a way to create a new favorite that is more a fruit pop than a sugar pop. Feel free to combine any fresh fruit with the grape juice to create new flavors.

2 cups white grape juice

1 cup raspberries

Pour the juice into popsicle molds until they are ⅔ full. Plastic popsicle molds can be purchased in most grocery stores. Each pop holds about 2 to 3 ounces. If you don't have a store-bought mold, a small paper cup and a plastic spoon or wooden popsicle stick can be used instead.

Place in the freezer for 1 hour. Drop a few berries into each mold until the liquid reaches just below the rim. Place the handles into the mold and freeze for another 2 hours. To remove the popsicle, run warm water over the mold until it loosens and pulls free.

Upside-Down Cherries and Berries Cake

SERVES 6 TO 8

MY DAD, AS MANY OF YOU ALREADY KNOW, loved to bake. And if he were still around today, this is a recipe I'm sure he'd love. He really enjoyed experimenting in the kitchen and would have liked using berries and especially fresh cherries instead of the traditional canned pineapple in this upside-down cake.

⅓ cup unsalted butter

½ cup dark brown sugar

2 cups halved pitted cherries

1 cup berries (such as raspberries or blackberries)

1⅓ cups sifted flour

1 cup sugar

2 teaspoons baking powder

½ teaspoon salt

¼ teaspoon ground cloves

½ teaspoon ground cinnamon

⅓ cup unsalted butter, cut into small cubes

⅔ cup heavy cream

2 teaspoons vanilla extract

1 egg, lightly beaten

Preheat the oven to 350°F.

Melt the butter in a 9-inch cast-iron skillet over medium heat. Remove from the heat and sprinkle evenly with the brown sugar. Place the cherries, cut side up, on the bottom of the pan. Fill in all the gaps with the berries. Set aside.

Put the flour, sugar, baking powder, salt, cloves and cinnamon in the bowl of an electric mixer fitted with a paddle. Working on low speed, slowly add the butter and cream. When blended, scrape down the bowl and then continue mixing on medium speed for 2 minutes. Add the vanilla extract and egg, scrape down once or twice and blend well.

Pour the batter evenly over the fruit and bake for 1 hour, until the edges pull from the sides of the skillet. Remove to a wire rack and cool in the skillet for 5 minutes. Gently bang the bottom of the pan on a hard surface and loosen the edges with a sharp knife. Place a large plate on top of the skillet and flip over. Lift off the skillet and readjust any fruit that has come loose. Cool and serve with a dollop of whipped cream.

White Russian Berries

WHILE I'M NOT A BIG FAN of coffee in the morning, I could drink ice coffee all day long. Kahlúa, a coffee liqueur, adds a nice punch to this dessert that tastes like a cross between iced coffee, a white Russian drink and a chunky smoothie. Be sure to let this sit in the refrigerator a bit to allow the flavors to combine.

1   pint blueberries

1   pint strawberries, hulled, chopped

½   pint raspberries

1   cup Kahlúa

½   cup heavy cream

2   tablespoons minced fresh mint

Gently mix all of the ingredients in a small bowl. Cover and refrigerate for 2 to 4 hours. Serve over ice cream, with a dollop of whipped cream, or atop a piece of cake.

Warm Summer Berries on Sorbet

SERVES 4

THERE'S SOMETHING ABOUT THE WARMTH of a sauce on the coolness of ice cream that makes my mouth water. It's the flip side of ice cream on warm apple pie. But don't limit yourself to dessert with this sauce. My daughter Taylor is currently in love with waffles every morning, and this makes a terrific, healthful addition to, or substitution for, maple syrup. It also makes a great topping for pound cakes, and adds a fruity texture to coffee cakes.

⅓ cup water

¼ cup pure maple syrup

⅛ teaspoon ground cinnamon

2 cups mixed berries (such as blueberries, raspberries, huckleberries or blackberries)

1 pint lemon sorbet

Bring the water, maple syrup and cinnamon to a boil in a medium-size pot. Add the berries and stir well. Simmer and stir for 3 to 5 minutes. The berries should break up a little, releasing some juice.

Scoop the sorbet into 4 glass goblets. Spoon the syrupy berries on top and serve.

Index